HERE COMES A CHOPPER TO CHOP OFF YOUR HEAD

THE DARK SIDE OF CHILDHOOD RHYMES AND STORIES

LIZ EVERS

metro

Published by Metro Publishing
an imprint of John Blake Publishing Ltd
3 Bramber Court, 2 Bramber Road,
London W14 9PB, England

www.johnblakepublishing.co.uk

www.facebook.com/johnblakebooks 🔳
twitter.com/jblakebooks 🔳

First published in hardback in 2014

ISBN: 978-1-78418-013-3

British Library Cataloguing-in-Publication Data:

A catalogue record for this book is available from the British Library.

Design by www.envydesign.co.uk

Cover illustration by Andrew Pinder

Printed in Great Britain by CPI Group (UK) Ltd

1 3 5 7 9 10 8 6 4 2

Papers used by John Blake Publishing are natural, recyclable products made from
wood grown in sustainable forests. The manufacturing processes conform
to the environmental regulations of the country of origin.

Every attempt has been made to contact the relevant copyright-holders, but some
were unobtainable. We would be grateful if the appropriate people could contact us.

HERE COMES
A CHOPPER
TO CHOP OFF
YOUR HEAD

HERE COMES A CHOPPER TO CHOP OFF YOUR HEAD

THE DARK SIDE OF CHILDHOOD RHYMES AND STORIES

LIZ EVERS

For Kate Power

ACKNOWLEDGEMENTS

Many thanks to my editor Anna Marx and all at John Blake.

Thanks also (and apologies for the months of neglect) to my friends and family, in particular Aoife Herrity, Kate O'Malley, Sarah-May O'Sullivan, Lorna Evers, Meabh Smith, Silvia Crompton and Patricia Evers who shared their fairy-tale memories (and occasional traumas).

And big thanks too to Fiona Dillon and Peter Evers for their support and diversions throughout.

Final thanks go to my nieces and nephews: Sean, Conor, Ruairí, Justin, Ben, Isabel, Lucy and Tom – and especially to Kate, whose penchant for nursery rhymes and demands for stories kick-started this project.

CONTENTS

INTRODUCTION

Two events led me to write this book – and both come from the same source, my niece Kate, who is seven at time of writing.

The first occurred a few years ago when I heard Kate, then a toddler, singing along to a CD of nursery rhymes. *Oranges and Lemons* was her favourite, and she demanded that it be played over and again. I knew the tune (infantilised in this version on a tinkling xylophone) but didn't remember the words from my own childhood. As I listened I was rather surprised to hear the last lines:

> 'Here comes the candle to light you to bed,
> Here comes a chopper to chop off your head.'

I did a little research and had my suspicions confirmed – this was a rhyme about execution. It seemed very strange

1

indeed to hear a little child singing along oblivious to the darkness of those lyrics.

I researched further, starting with the nursery rhymes I knew best – and found that many of them were either overtly gruesome (Bo-Peep's lambs having their tails chopped off, ditto the *Three Blind Mice*, the blackbird pecking off the maid's nose in *Sing a Song of Sixpence*, etc., etc.) or had an even darker message and history behind them.

Hugely varied in their origins, any child's treasury of nursery rhymes reads like an A to Z of the macabre – from pagan superstitions and rituals including human sacrifice (*London Bridge is Falling Down, Eeny, Meeny, Miny, Mo*), to miscarried babies (*Mary, Mary, Quite Contrary*), to the persecution of Catholics (*Goosey, Goosey Gander*), to torturing animals (*Ding Dong Bell, Pussy's in the Well*) to child battery (*There Was an Old Woman Who Lived in a Shoe*).

The second event that led me to write this book was in fact less one event than a series of events. As she grew older, Kate started to ask to be told stories, preferably ones made up on the spot. I found that the impromptu silly stories I spun always had a fairy-tale quality – wicked witches, talking animals, monstrous creatures and trepidation galore. I wondered at the urge to finesse the stories with scary details, and started to wonder too at the influence of the stories I had read, or had read to me, as a child.

2

INTRODUCTION

I remembered how my favourite tales were populated with frightening figures set on persecuting innocents – the grotesque stepsisters of *Cinderella*, the sinister goblin-like spinner of *Rumpelstiltskin*, and the evil maid in *The Goose Girl* who steals the identity of a beautiful princess, murders her beloved horse and forces her into servitude. Time had blurred the 'happy endings' of these stories and all that was left was a pervading sense of menace.

I then asked friends and family what they remembered about the fairy tales they heard as children, and, indeed, if they themselves shared these stories with their own offspring.

My mother, Patricia, remarked: 'I always thought they were weird. Even when I was reading them to my children I thought they were weird. Why I persisted, I don't know.'

While my friend Aoife described the fairy tale *Bluebeard* as a 'game-changer', saying 'I'll never forget reading that, it scared the crap out of me!'

Another friend Sarah-May told me she's still haunted by *The Little Mermaid* to this day: 'Every time I'm at a beach or by the sea I think of her disappearing into the foam.'

And my friend Kate described a rather awkward moment that arose when reading *Snow White* to her four-year-old daughter Meabh: 'My mam had been reading her an "edited" version of *Snow White* in advance of us going to see the pantomime at Christmas. I wasn't aware of this and, the day before going, I read her the whole

3

unsanitised version – dagger, woods, heart in a box – the lot.

'Meabh's eyes widened and I realised I'd just told my daughter about murder for the first time... and not an average one at that. She did enjoy the panto though and I felt that, at least when that guy was packing the foam dagger in his backpack for the walk in the woods, she was in the loop!'

Digging deeper, I again found that, while the so-called 'sanitised' versions of the fairy tales I knew as a child were already pretty scary and strange, the stories behind the stories where often utterly terrifying.

I read the 'original' version of *Sleeping Beauty*, for example, written in 1697 by the French author Charles Perrault. I never knew there was a second half to this already peculiar tale about cursing little girls – a spectacularly gruesome finale involving a cannibalistic mother-in-law intent on eating Sleeping Beauty and her two infant children (while the stories that informed it were laced with rape and necrophilia).

Then there were *Little Red Riding Hood*'s forebears – cautionary tales about child molesters – awash with gore; the brutality of the *Cinderella* story, with her cruel sisters chopping off bits of their feet in the hope of squeezing them into the enchanted slipper; the fate of Snow White's cannibalistic stepmother, made to dance to death in red-hot iron shoes; the extraordinary violence of *Hansel and*

Gretel's forebear *Hop o' my Thumb* in which seven little girls have their throats cut; and the unspeakable backstory to the already unspeakable tale of *Bluebeard*, based on a serial killer who dispatched hundreds of children in ways too vicious and depraved to repeat.

The more I read, the more intrigued I became – just where did these rhymes and fairy tales come from – and what was their enduring appeal?

Once upon a time

> 'Fairy tales represent hundreds of years of stories based on thousands of years of stories told by hundreds, thousands, perhaps even millions of tellers.'
> – Kate Bernheimer, fairy-tale scholar

Most of the fairy tales in the 'canon' – that is the ones most commonly collected together – were popularised by the French writer Charles Perrault in the late seventeenth century, the German brothers Wilhelm and Jacob Grimm in the early nineteenth and Danish writer Hans Christian Andersen in the mid-nineteenth century. And these in turn drew on multiple sources – earlier tales from the oral folklore traditions of not only France, Germany and Scandinavia, but also across the European continent from Russia all the way to Italy and Greece, and with variations found much further east – from ancient Persia and India.

We can never know whether or not one early cultural group was responsible for originating and spreading these tales. Many existed for millennia in oral form passed from generation to generation, and country to country. It was with the advent of print that the 'canon' of tales became a little more fixed and – though the tales we know today still continue to evolve and have multiple variations – the set list has now become familiar.

We can certainly trace the nearer written origins of many of the tales to stories by the Italian writers Gianfrancesco Straparola (1480–1557) and Giambattista Basile (1566–1632).

Straparola was the author of the first notable collection of European (specifically, Italian) fairy tales, *The Facetious Nights of Straparola* (1550–53). Printed in two volumes, this collection featured seventy-five extraordinary tales, many of which were later adapted by Basile, Perrault and the Grimms.

Published posthumously, Basile's *Pentamerone* (1634–36, also known as *Lo cunto de li cunti overo lo trattenemiento de peccerille* – 'The Tale of Tales, or Entertainment for Little Ones') was a collection of oral tales, chiefly from Crete and Venice. These built on many of Straparola's tales, and brought 'new' ones to light. In the *Pentamerone* we find early versions of some of our most familiar tales including *Cinderella*, *Puss in Boots*, *Sleeping Beauty* and *Rapunzel*.

Folk and fairy tales became something of a craze in

the literary salons of late seventeenth-century Paris. In fact, it was there that the phrase 'fairy tale' or *conte de fée* was coined by one Madame d'Aulnoy – an avid collector and teller of tales. The genre was a very female one, originating with groups of genteel women, known as the *précieuses* (from a literary style deriving from conversation and playful word games), who gathered to show off their storytelling prowess. The sources of their tales were a combination of the literary and the folk (told by servants or women of the lower classes). These fairy tales, in the context of the salon, were told by adults to other adults.

But with the publication of his 1697 *Tales and Stories of the Past with Morals* (*Histoires ou Contes du Temps passé*), subtitled *Tales of Mother Goose* (*Les Contes de ma Mère l'Oye*), salon regular Charles Perrault (1628–1703) took ownership of the genre to all intents and purposes – and made children his target audience. Four of the eleven tales that appear in his one and only fairy-tale collection take pride of place in the established canon: *Little Red Riding Hood*, *Cinderella*, *Puss in Boots* and *Sleeping Beauty*, while other more adult-themed ones like *Bluebeard* and *Donkey Skin* lurk at the peripheries.

Another classic tale coming from this literary movement in France is *Beauty and the Beast*, first published as *La Belle et la Bête* in 1740 by Gabrielle-Suzanne Barbot de Villeneuve (1695–1755), then abridged and retold to great acclaim by Jeanne-Marie Le Prince de Beaumont in 1756.

While many may not be familiar with the name Charles Perrault, the Brothers Grimm have long since achieved international fame for their collections of fairy and folk tales. The Brothers collected oral folk tales, usually from middle-class German ladies, with something of a nationalist agenda. While their first collection *Children's and Household Tales*, published in 1812, featured tales from non-German sources, these were expunged from later editions. And not only that, but they rewrote some of the tales and cut the more disturbing ones to make them more palatable to a wider audience and a little easier for children to digest. I've noted some of the more significant shifts in content and tone from the 1812 originals to the later versions of some of the tales explored in this book.

The Grimms made the biggest contribution to the fairy-tale canon, additionally enshrining *Hansel and Gretel*, *Snow White*, *Rapunzel*, *Rumpelstiltskin*, *The Frog King/Prince*, *The Wolf and Seven Young Kids* and others too numerous to list here.

The Grimms created a huge interest in folklore and story collection, kick-starting something of an industry that inspired others from Japan, India, Russia, Norway, Scotland, Ireland and many other countries to record and collate their own oral tales.

In the mid-nineteenth century, Hans Christian Andersen perfected the literary fairy tale – original stories that augmented or appropriated pre-existing folklore or were entirely his own invention. Andersen's tales had a clearer moral purpose, addressing issues of class and sympathising with the marginalised and persecuted.

With Andersen came *The Emperor's New Clothes*, *The Snow Queen*, *The Little Match Girl*, *The Little Mermaid*, *Thumbelina*, *The Princess and the Pea*, *The Brave Tin Soldier*, *The Ugly Duckling* and many, many more.

Fairy tales became quite the craze in England too, with one of the most notable collectors, Joseph Jacobs (1854–1916), adding uniquely English tales to the canon such as *The Story of the Three Bears*, *Jack and the Beanstalk*, *Jack the Giant Killer*, *The History of Tom Thumb* and *Whittington and His Cat*.

Contrary rhymes

What we now call 'nursery rhymes' are in fact an assortment of short poems, riddles, songs and lullabies from folk and popular culture of Britain and, to a lesser extent, America. Many date back hundreds of years and their origins and meanings can only be guessed at.

The first collection that led to their being seen as a collective genre aimed at a younger audience was *Tommy Thumb's Song Book*, published in the 1740s. It was first advertised in the *London Evening Post* in March 1744 as being 'for all little Masters and Misses, to be sung to them by their Nurses till they can sing themselves'. While no original copy of the song book survives, rhymes featuring in subsequent reprints include *Pat-a-Cake*, *Baby on a Tree*

Top (better known as *Rock/Hush-a-Bye Baby*) and *London Bridge is Falling Down*.

Prior to that, these rhymes, songs and riddles were disseminated to a wider audience through 'chapbooks'. Published since the sixteenth century, chapbooks were pamphlets usually consisting of a single sheet of paper folded into books of between eight and twenty-four pages and featuring everything from ballads, songs, popular folk stories, rhymes, riddles and poetry, to political and religious tracts. London was the hub of print production – producing huge volumes that were distributed throughout the city and country. It is no surprise then that many rhymes were well known the length and breadth of the land, often spawning regional variations. Chapbooks remained hugely popular through to the eighteenth century.

Fragments of 'nursery rhymes' can also be found in literary texts, including those of William Shakespeare (1564–1616). Jack and Jill make an appearance in both *A Midsummer Night's Dream* and *Love's Labour's Lost*, for example. And a verse reminiscent of *Little Boy Blue* is found in *King Lear*, while the expression 'Ding dong bell' appears in both *The Tempest* and *The Merchant of Venice*.

Around 1765, publisher John Newbery, also known as 'the father of children's literature' published *Mother Goose's Melody* or *Sonnets for the Cradle* – which featured the well-known rhymes *Dickery, Dickery, Dock* and *See-Saw, Margery*

Daw. Again no copy of the original version exists. But an advertisement in the *London Chronicle* for a reprint in 1780 states that it contains 'the most celebrated songs and lullabies of the old British nurses; calculated to amuse children, and to excite them to sleep'.

Other 'song books' quickly followed, including the amusingly named *Nancy Cock's Pretty Song Book* (c. 1781) and *Tom Tit's Song Book* (1790).

Nursery rhymes exploded in popularity during the nineteenth century, especially during the Victorian period (1837–1901), in both Britain and North America. When Shakespearean scholar James Orchard Halliwell (1820–89) published *The Nursery Rhymes of England* in 1842 and *Popular Rhymes and Tales* in 1849, he effectively established the canon of popular nursery rhymes. And these collected verses or variations on them have been replicated in countless books since then.

Nursery Rhymes of England features such rhymes as *Pussy Cat, Pussy Cat, Where Have You Been?*, *Little Miss Mopsey* (a.k.a. Muffet), *There Was a Crooked Man*, *Little Jack Horner*, *There Was an Old Woman Who Lived in a Shoe*, *Three Blind Mice*, *Sing a Song of Sixpence*, *Old Mother Hubbard*, *Little Bo-Peep*, *Humpty Dumpty*, *Goosey, Goosey Gander*, *See a Pin and Pick it Up*, *Oranges and Lemons*, *Mistress Mary, Quite Contrary* (a.k.a. *Mary, Mary, Quite Contrary*), and many more.

HERE COMES A CHOPPER TO CHOP OFF YOUR HEAD

The times are a-changing

> 'In a utilitarian age, of all other times, it is a matter
> of grave importance that fairy tales should be
> respected.'   – Charles Dickens

A study carried out in 2013 by the makers of the musical
toy Symphony in B revealed that contemporary songs
are putting the squeeze on nursery rhymes and lullabies
– with a clear majority of the 2,000 parents interviewed
preferring to sing pop hits from Robbie Williams, Bruno
Mars, Adele and Rihanna to their little ones rather
than the more traditional fare. But, given the adult
theme of heartbreak that runs through most of these
contemporary songs, one might wonder which is 'better'
for impressionable young minds.

Another study from 2012 of 2,000 US parents was
commissioned to mark the launch of the TV drama series
Grimm, about a modern-day homicide detective gifted
with the ability to see the bloody-minded mythological
or 'fairy-tale' creatures who live among us.

The study revealed that one in five parents don't tell
their children fairy tales at all, and one third reported
their children had become upset by tales such as *Little
Red Riding Hood*. Parents were less likely to read their
children *Rumpelstiltskin* because it depicts kidnapping and
execution, ditto *Goldilocks and the Three Bears* because it

condones theft, and *Hansel and Gretel* was the least likely of all because it's just plain terrifying.

A quarter said they wouldn't read fairy stories to children under five because of the awkward questions that might arise. And half thought Cinderella was a poor role model – doing housework all day.

Childhood today is a very different thing to what it was in the not-too-distant past. Children's innocence is more prized and fretted about than ever before. Previously childhood would have been a considerably shorter affair, with children expected to work and contribute to the family – whether in the home, the family business or on the farm. It was the coming of the industrial revolution – with its heightened demand for child labour and the appalling conditions under which children were expected to work – that sparked the beginning of our Western notions of childhood as a longer, more precious time period. A popular movement emerged in the 1830s to stop child labour, with writers such as Charles Dickens among the prominent and influential voices.

These changes in the perception of our little lambs are directly related to the emergence of nursery rhymes and fairy tales as literary forms specifically for children.

What's inside…
As well as looking at the often fascinating backgrounds, historical contexts and sources of nursery rhymes and

fairy tales, this book explores the 'lessons' we learned from them as children – and how their often skewed morality prepared us for the big bad world outside. As I said at the outset, for me the 'happy ever after' element faded from memory long ago and only the residual scariness remained.

We'll see how nursery rhymes and fairy tales abound with superstitions and curses, making the mundane and everyday fearful for the young mind, and turning even wishing into a dangerous game. We'll also look at what they teach us about the adult world of sex and marriage; what they tell us about our leaders, history and class society; about crime and punishment; and about the family unit – think about all that child battery and abandonment, and those wicked stepfamilies for starters…

Above all, I hope reading this book takes you on a nostalgic journey, and perhaps even a revelatory one. You might identify where some of those long-held neuroses you have come from. I certainly did!

Liz Evers
Dublin, 2014

CHAPTER 1

SOWING SUPERSTITION: HOW TO TURN YOUR CHILD INTO A NEUROTIC

'Think what you would have been now, if instead of being fed with tales and old wives' fables in childhood, you had been crammed with geography and natural history!'
— Charles Lamb

In his book *The Uses of Enchantment: The Meaning and Importance of Fairy Tales* (1976), psychoanalyst Bruno Bettelheim (1903–90) tells us that the dark themes in fairy tales (e.g. death, abandonment and imprisonment) help children to cope with their fears in symbolic terms and support their emotional growth. He says the stories provide a reassurance that, though a process may be difficult, things will be all right in the end and that fears and anxieties can be overcome, i.e. that one can live 'happily ever after'.

But in my experience fairy tales taught me not that good would win out in the end and all would be well, but that bizarre misfortunes could befall me at any moment and that creatures with magical powers bent on my destruction lurked unseen in every corner. The rhymes I rhymed off turned everyday items, animals and birds into potential sources of danger and taught me that just one sneeze could portend my doom.

Basically, I learned that the world is a terrifying place, governed by strange and opaque rules with woe betiding those who, for example, had the audacity to cut their nails on a Sunday or find themselves in the presence of a lone magpie.

PART I: NURSERY RHYMES

ONE FOR SORROW

One for sorrow,
Two for joy,
Three for a girl,
Four for a boy,
Five for silver,
Six for gold,
Seven for a secret never to be told.

Thanks to this rhyme and the associated superstition, children (and adults) have long been fearful of the sight of a lone magpie, frantically looking for a second, third or fourth magpie to save them from 'bad luck'.

A member of the much-maligned crow family, magpies are considered bad omens – and references to this long-standing superstition can be found from the sixteenth century onwards, in Western cultures anyway. In China and Korea, the magpie is seen as a symbol of good luck and good fortune.

Magpies are best known for stealing things, killing smaller birds and mimicking other birds' calls (well rattley, harsh-sounding ones anyway). The character of the thieving magpie shows up in the folklore of countries including Italy, France, Bulgaria, the Czech Republic, Germany, Hungary, Poland and Sweden.

They are also associated with witchcraft in Britain. In Yorkshire, you might make the sign of the cross to ward off the evil associated with this pariah bird. While, in Scotland, a lone magpie lurking near the window of a house is meant to portend the passing of one of the inhabitants. And throughout England greeting the lone bird with 'Good morning/afternoon/evening, Mr Magpie, how is your lady wife today?' is considered a safeguard against ill fortune.

Legend has it that the magpie was the only bird that didn't sing to comfort Jesus on the cross. What comfort their rattling caw would have brought is another thing.

I had never understood why one magpie on its own would be bad luck or a source or sorrow. And why this misfortune could be negated by a few of the magpie's friends showing up. But then a superstition-loving friend told me about the rhyme's melancholic nature. Magpies mate for life – so, if you see one on its own, something unpleasant may have befallen its other half or, indeed, it may not yet have found its magpie love.

The best-known version of the rhyme counts just seven magpies. But there are many different versions of the *One for Sorrow* rhyme, some of them going as high as twenty magpies.

The very first recorded version of the rhyme is in John Brand's *Observations on Popular Antiquities* published in 1780. It is short and bleak:

> One for sorrow,
> Two for mirth,
> Three for a wedding,
> And four for death.

In some versions 'death' is swapped for 'birth', changing the meaning substantially to make a rhyme with 'mirth'.

The devil makes an appearance in some variations of the rhyme. In MA Denham's *Proverbs and Popular Saying of the Seasons* (1846), we find:

One for sorrow,
Two for luck,
Three for a wedding,
Four for death,
Five for silver,
Six for gold,
Seven for a secret,
Not to be told,
Eight for heaven,
Nine for hell,
And ten for the devil's own self!

Which has subsequently been shortened to:

One for sorrow
Two for mirth
Three for a funeral
Four for a birth
Five for heaven
Six for hell
Seven's the Devil his own self.

A version from Manchester adds the following additional lines to the usual seven, linking the devil with the number thirteen, maxing out the superstition quota for one rhyme:

Eight for a wish
Nine for a kiss
Ten a surprise you should be careful not to miss
Eleven for health
Twelve for wealth
Thirteen beware it's the devil himself.

Putting aside this cruel abuse, magpies are thought to be not just one of the most intelligent birds, but one of the most intelligent creatures in the world – with an impressive brain that is big in all the right places. As well as being adept thieves and clever enough to hide from their predators, there are accounts of magpies opening locks, working together in groups (to fend off a cat for example) and even rescuing their own kind by communal airlifting to safety. They also build nests of twigs with a domed roof to protect them from predators (and presumably stash their stolen jewels).

A further superstitious proverb about magpies is found in the wildly popular 1840s book *A Guide to the Scientific Knowledge of Things Familiar* by Ebenezer Cobham Brewer: 'A single magpie in spring, foul weather will bring'.

THIS LITTLE PIG WENT TO MARKET

One for Sorrow is just one of many 'counting rhymes'. My favourite as a child was the 'Little Piggy' toe-counting rhyme, which involved gleeful foot tickling at the end. Thankfully, the rhyme I recall had a happier ending than the first printed version, which appeared in James Orchard Halliwell's *The Nursery Rhymes of England* in 1842:

> This little pig went to market;
> This little pig staid at home;
> This little pig had a bit of bread and butter;
> This little pig had none;
> This little pig said, Wee, wee, wee!
> I can't find my way home. ['All the way home'
> in later, happier versions]

Another version in the same book sees one of the pigs' mothers meet a rather unusual end:

> Let us go to the wood, says this pig;
> What to do there? says that pig;
> To look for my mother, says this pig;
> What to do with her? says that pig;
> Kiss her to death, says this pig.

A Nightmare on Elm Street
Counting rhymes don't get creepier than the one that featured in the 1984 horror movie *A Nightmare on Elm Street*. It is based on the innocent original *One, Two, Buckle My Shoe* (first published 1805), which involves nothing more

sinister than a 'big fat hen' at the end. The film version is sung by otherworldly little girls in white matching dresses playing jump-rope. We presume they are one-time victims of the burned-faced, knife-fingered Freddy Krueger. Their alternate lyrics run:

> One, two,
> Freddy's coming for you.
> Three, four,
> Better lock your door.
> Five, six,
> Grab a crucifix.
> Seven, eight,
> Better stay up late.
> Nine, ten,
> Never sleep again.

SEE A PIN

> See a pin and pick it up,
> All the day you'll have good luck.
> See a pin and let it lay,
> Bad luck you'll have all the day.

This is a considerably nicer rhyme, albeit another that breeds superstition in the young, impressionable mind.

Pins were a relatively expensive item a few hundred

years ago. So much so that in 1543 King Henry VIII passed an act banning the importation of pins from outside his kingdom in an effort to encourage more to be manufactured domestically. And these pins had to be of a certain quality too: 'no person shall put to sale any pinnes but only such as shall be double headed, and have the heads soldered fast to the shank of the pinnes, well smoothed, the shank well shapen, the points well and round filed, canted and sharpened'.

If a married woman needed to buy them, she might ask her husband for 'pin money'. So finding such an item by chance was indeed quite a lucky thing, and ignoring one a little foolhardy.

The rhyme has morphed into 'See a penny pick it up', which is more relevant to a contemporary audience – imbuing pennies with an extra good fortune not linked to their face value.

Pins are linked with several good and bad luck superstitions. A pin left in a wedding dress is thought to be very unlucky and to be prescient of ill fortune for the marriage ahead. Also, a pin found on a ship was feared by sailors as a potential source of a leak. On the other hand, pins were once thought to protect a household against witchcraft if stuck in a doorframe or placed under the floorboards.

Pins, needles and warts
When I was a child, my family used to go on Sunday outings to a place called Trim in County Meath in Ireland. The town is home to a once grand Norman castle as well as the impressive ruins of the thirteenth-century monastery, Newtown Abbey. In a graveyard near the monastery is the altar tomb of Sir Lucas Dillion and his wife Lady Jane Bathe, locally known as the 'Jealous Man and Woman'. This sixteenth-century couple are so named because of the sword that menacingly divides their reposing stone figures. Local legend has it that, if you leave a pin in one of the many rainwater puddles that gather on the tomb, any warts you have will disappear.

On a recent nostalgic visit to Trim, I saw that my old weather-beaten, ruff-wearing stone friends were still in situ. A great number of rusty, good luck pins fill the space between them, alongside the jealous sword.

LADYBIRD, LADYBIRD

Ladybird, ladybird, fly away home,
Your house is on fire and your children are gone,
All except one who is called little Ann,
For she crept under the frying pan.

This rhyme conjured rather terrifying images for me as a child. I imagined a distraught ladybird learning that her home was ablaze and her children 'gone' – I assumed burned to death – while little Ann cowered under a frying pan for safety as the flames licked ever closer...

Others may not have had the same panic-stricken reaction. And in another version of the rhyme it states that the children have 'flown' so have presumably escaped death by burning.

The rhyme was first published in 1865 but certainly predates that by at least 200 years, if not longer.

It is considered good luck to have a ladybird land on you, and killing one is bad luck. The ladybird has long been a friend to the farmer and gardener, eating aphids (green fly) and thus protecting their crops. So one explanation for the rhyme is that it serves as a gentle warning to ladybirds to leave the land at the end of the harvest when stubble may be set on fire to make way for the next crop. This rhyme is meant to be recited to one that lands on you before blowing it gently from your finger to help it on its way.

So far, so benevolent.

However, one theory of origin links the rhyme to the persecution of Catholics. Ladybirds represent the Virgin Mary ('Our Lady') or otherwise have holy connections in religious traditions in Britain, Ireland, Germany, Spain and France.

It is thought that the rhyme may serve as a warning to Catholics who refused to attend Protestant services in mid-sixteenth century Britain. This persecuted group instead conducted clandestine masses away from prying eyes, but those caught attending or officiating would face severe recrimination, including burning at the stake. There will be lots more on rhymes about the brutalising of Catholics by various British monarchs to follow in Chapter 3.

But none of this explains little Ann under the frying pan.

It would appear that Ann is a relic from some older rhyme still. Her name appears in a German version of the rhyme, which is quite similar to the English.

JACK BE NIMBLE

Jack be nimble,
Jack be quick,
Jack jump over
The candlestick.

Way back whenever (the rhyme was first published in 1798 but is of much older origin), jumping over a candlestick was supposedly a way of telling fortunes. The outcomes were pretty limited – if you jumped over it and the candle stayed alight, then good luck would be yours all year. If the candle went out... bad luck. This odd ritual was usually performed at Christmas time or at weddings.

The jumping theme makes it an ideal companion for children's skipping games, especially when you include the additional verse:

Jack jumped high,
Jack jumped low,
Jack jumped over
And burned his toe.

So, on the surface, this is a relatively light-hearted little ditty about not much of anything – unless the candle goes out on your wedding day that is (and heaven forbid a pin is found in the bride's dress on the day too, see pin superstitions p23). But candle-leaping has its origin in the pagan tradition of fire-leaping to ward off evil spirits. Fires would have contained animal bones as an additional symbol of sacrifice to keep wickedness at bay. And indeed the word 'bonfire' (bone-fire) is thought to be derived from this practice.

Other theories of origin link the rhyme to the equally charming subjects of disease and piracy.

Yellow fever, also known as Yellow Jack, is a very dangerous and highly infectious disease which was rife in Europe from the seventeenth to the early twentieth century – and according to lore the feverish symptoms could be drawn out of the body with the heat of a good fire. It was also believed that the presence of a fire or candle could ward off the disease, and so, during epidemics, candles might be lit to keep the disease away from children – hence the connection with the rhyme.

Another theory of origin relates to a pirate called Calico Jack Rackham who did his marauding in the late seventeenth and early eighteenth centuries. Known for his colourful clothing, Calico Jack's supposed quick-wittedness and nimble ways kept him out of the hands of the law – for a while anyway. He was eventually caught, and executed. Other sources say the nimble, law-evading pirate was one Black Jack, whose marauding took place in the sixteenth century.

CUT YOUR NAILS ON MONDAY

Cut your nails on Monday, cut them for news;
Cut them on Tuesday, a pair of new shoes;
Cut them on Wednesday, cut them for health;
Cut them on Thursday, cut them for wealth;
Cut them on Friday, cut them for woe;
Cut them on Saturday, a journey you'll go;
Cut them on Sunday, you'll cut them for evil,
For all the next week you'll be ruled by the devil.

This version is from *The Home Book of Verse, Vol 1* edited by Burton Egbert Stevenson (1912). There are a few versions of this rhyme with different things associated with the different days, but cutting your nails on Sunday is always a bad thing to do. Friday's not great either.

In Japan, cutting your finger- or toenails at night is bad luck. And the bad luck is very specific. Clipping those nails in the evening may mean you will not be with your parents at their deathbeds.

I've heard tell of an old English superstition about not cutting a baby's nails before the age of one as it is meant to be bad luck. I suspect, however, that's just an excuse to chew off babies' fingernails, which, while it might sound a little disgusting, can be preferable to the nerve-wracking experience of using a clippers or scissors to trim the nails on those tiny, dainty fingers.

There is a very similar rhyme for sneezing, which also promises sorrow on a Friday and being bedevilled for a week if you're silly enough to sneeze on a Sunday.

RING-A-RING O' ROSES

Ring-a-ring o' roses,
A pocket full of posies,
Atishoo! Atishoo!
We all fall down.

Continuing the sneezing theme, this nursery rhyme has been around since at least the late eighteenth century, with similar versions in other European languages. It first appeared in print in 1881 and since the middle of the twentieth century has been associated with the 'Great Plague' of 1665 or even the Black Death of the 1340s. Sneezing and falling down are obvious signs of illness. It has further been suggested that the 'ring o' roses' is a red rash associated with the plague and that posies were used to cover the smell of the disease.

But modern folklorists reject this interpretation, chiefly because the symptoms don't match the disease. But whether they do or not, the rhyme has now been shared with several generations of children, including mine, in the belief that it was about the plague – and that's enough for me in terms of strange traditions to pass down to your children.

There are multiple variations of it from both England and America (including those with neither sneezing nor falling down involved).

The version above is now the standard one and children dance to it in a circle, holding hands and swinging their arms before falling to the ground 'dead' with a dramatic flourish at the end.

While the plague interpretation has been discredited, there is no strong contending explanation, so it seems likely that the myth of disease will continue – and parents will intentionally teach their kids to act out this cute little dying game for the foreseeable.

In 1949, a parody of the rhyme appeared in *The Observer* newspaper in Britain, making macabre use of its association with death:

> Ring-a-ring o' geranium,
> A pocket full of uranium.
> Hiro, shima,
> All fall down.

Bless You

People have reportedly been saying 'bless you' to each other for sneezes since the first century.

Consequently, when the bubonic plague ripped through Europe in the late sixth century, it is said that the new Pope, Gregory I (540–604), ordered perpetual prayer in the streets and that blessings were dished out in the hope of quelling the disease.

Another rather bizarre and implausible explanation for offering a blessing is that it was once believed that the soul might be thrown from the body with a forceful sneeze and so the blessing was an attempt to prevent such a catastrophe.

Internationally, there are lots of variations on the 'bless you' reaction to sneezing – most common is a wish for good health. However, in Mongolian, as well as some

Muslim traditions, a sneezer is greeted with a rather ominous 'May God forgive you'.

PART II: FAIRY TALES

Fairy tales may not always contain fairies, but when they do they are often creatures rooted in ancient superstitions – bringing either good fortune or ill – bearing curses or spells, or the remedies to curses or spells.

As a child growing up in Ireland, I was inducted into the myriad superstitions surrounding fairies or the 'good people' (you have to call them that or they'll hurt you). Being from urban Dublin, I was spared the worst of these superstitions, but friends from more remote, rural parts of the country were fairly saturated in fairy lore growing up.

To this day, there are superstitions around Banshees, female fairies whose crying or 'keening' at night foretells death of a family member. Then there's the untouchability of so-called 'fairy forts' or 'fairy rings', which are the bumpy overgrown earth works of long-fallen houses or village enclosures, or ancient burial mounds, beneath which fairies are said to live – and tampering with them brings either a terrible curse or death. There are fairy trees – usually hawthorn, ash or oak – similarly said to house the malevolent 'good' people and thus must be treated with reverence and care so as not to invoke the wrath of their inhabitants.

Such superstitions are not unique to Ireland, it's just that they are still very much alive there. The one thing you must never do is the same across all cultures where fairy lore is still remembered – you must never, ever, cause offence to the fairies. If you want proof just ask Sleeping Beauty's parents...

SLEEPING BEAUTY

The curse of an offended fairy is at the heart of this tale, first published as *Sleeping Beauty in the Wood* by Charles Perrault in 1697. Unlike many of the other fairy tales in this book, *Sleeping Beauty* doesn't have widespread folk roots. The only other close version we know of is *Sun, Moon and Talia* by Giambattista Basile, which is very obviously the inspiration for Perrault's tale and which in turn was likely to have been inspired by a fourteenth-century French romance called *Perceforce*. And then of course there's the highly sanitised *Briar Rose* version by the Brothers Grimm – which is the one most children would be familiar with from fairy-tale anthologies.

In Perrault's version, a king and queen long desperately for a child. When they eventually manage to have one – a beautiful baby girl – the overjoyed king decides to host an elaborate celebration in her honour. Wanting the very best start in life for his little treasure, the king invites all the fairies of the land to attend the party so they might bestow gifts upon the baby girl. There are seven fairies in the land and all are invited, come and duly start dishing out their gifts – beauty, cleverness, grace, dancing prowess, the ability to sing like a nightingale and musicality. Six of the seven have dispensed their gifts when an eighth fairy, a somewhat deranged curmudgeon, shows up. Everyone had believed her to be long dead as she hadn't been seen outside of the tower she lives in for fifty years.

This eighth fairy feels snubbed and offended and so curses the unfortunate infant to die by a prick of a spindle on her hand at an unspecified time in the future.

Having condemned the child to death (again, you really should never offend a fairy), the old woman trundles off on her unhappy way. Thankfully, there is one fairy left who has yet to bestow a gift upon the child, and, though she can't undo the magic of another fairy, she can mitigate it a little. So she changes the spell so that the little girl will not die by the prick of a spindle, but instead will fall into a deep sleep, one hundred years long – and be awakened by the son of a king.

To try to safeguard his child from all spindle-related accidents, the king immediately orders every such device banned from his kingdom on pain of death.

Sixteen gloriously spindle-free years pass and the unnamed princess grows into a beautiful young woman. Then one day, when the king and queen are away and the princess is free to roam the castle, she visits a high tower she has never been to before where she finds an old woman spinning away with a spindle. This old dear is unaware of the blanket ban on such activity and happily tries to induct the princess into the art of spinning – with dire consequences. The girl immediately pricks her finger on the spindle and falls into a deep sleep.

The fairy who previously altered the curse to lesser curse status arrives shortly thereafter and places everyone else in the castle under a sleeping spell, including the animals and even the fires too. Everyone except the king and queen that is, who sorrowfully decide to abandon their castle for good, but, before they do, they lay out their treasured daughter on a bed embroidered with silver and gold.

Trees and briars soon engulf the unattended castle park, making it impassable. One hundred years go by and on the day the curse expires a young prince is out hunting nearby, he's heard stories of the strange castle and its beautiful, sleeping inhabitant and decides, against the advice of the locals, to investigate. As he approaches, the wall of forbidding briars parts for him (he's clearly 'the one') – he enters, passes the various slumbering inhabitants and heads to the room that houses the sleeping princess. Needless to say when he sees her laid out all silver and gold as if just asleep, he falls for her instantly. He kneels by her side (no kiss)

35

and she awakens. The first thing she says, 'Is that you, my prince? What a long time you have kept me waiting.' The two lovers chat for four hours, while the rest of the castle inhabitants awaken, utterly famished.

The prince has the decency not to point out to the newly awakened princess that she is dressed 'like Grandmother in the old days'. The two dine together in a hall full of mirrors and are married that very night.

The curse has been lifted and at this point you might expect the '...and they lived happily ever after' line, but it will not be forthcoming. Perrault's is a story of two halves. While later tellings end on the marriage, there is a second half here that takes the reader to a rather unexpected place – one characterised by treachery, terror and cannibalism.

So, the two are married but the prince doesn't want to take his new bride back to his own kingdom because he's afraid of his mother. She's part-ogre and pretty unpredictable. We learn that the prince's father only married her for her money. So the prince keeps his marriage secret for four whole years, flitting between kingdoms and having two children Dawn, a girl, and Day, a boy, with his wife in the interim. Eventually, when his father dies and he must take over as king, he finds the courage to tell his fearsome mother all about his secret life, wife and children.

He moves his young family into his own castle but

is soon called off to fight a war with a neighbouring kingdom. He leaves his mother in charge, asking her to look after his wife and children. No sooner is he out of the picture than his mother's ogress ways come to the fore. Immediately, she whisks her daughter-in-law and two grandchildren off to her summer residence in the forest and starts to implement a ghoulish plan – she wants to eat them, one by one.

The queen instructs her reluctant steward to first kill her granddaughter Dawn and serve her up in an onion and mustard sauce. The poor man thus instructed finds the little four-year-old girl but can't bring himself to kill her, so instead he hides her in his house with his wife and kills and cooks a lamb instead. The queen eats the meal with great relish, saying she's never eaten anything that tasted so good.

The following week, she says she wants little Day for dinner and so the steward again hides the child and serves the cannibal queen a young goat instead.

And then, finally it's her daughter-in-law's turn to be eaten. The steward resolves that there is no way out of this one; the princess is older, and tougher, than her children and so cannot be easily substituted with the flesh of another animal. But when he faces the princess and tells her of her fate his heart melts and instead he kills a doe to serve to the queen, reuniting the young family in secrecy.

Quite sated with her evil doings, the queen plans to tell her son that 'ravening' wolves did away with his wife and children. But before leaving her forest residence, she hears Day crying in the steward's house and the rest of the family trying to silence him and realises she has been deceived. The next day, she orders a huge cauldron to be brought into the courtyard and filled with toads and snakes into which she plans to throw her daughter-in-law, her grandchildren and those who aided and abetted them. Just as she is about to commit this gruesome deed, her son arrives to save the day. Only he doesn't save it – instead, his mother throws herself into the cauldron of her own volition and is there devoured by all the horrible slithering things inside.

Do they live happily ever after? Perrault doesn't say. We only learn that the king is upset because, even though she was a cannibalistic ogre, the queen was his mother. And that he was 'consoled' by his beautiful wife and children. Frankly, I think they got the raw deal in this one and should be the ones receiving consolation.

Perrault included a 'moral' at the end of each of his tales, and make of this one what you will:

For girls to wait awhile, so they may wed
A loving husband, handsome, rich and kind:
That's natural enough, I'd say;
But just the same, to stay in bed
A hundred years asleep – you'll never find

Such patience in a girl today.
Another lesson may be meant:
Lovers lose nothing if they wait,
And tie the knot of marriage late;
They'll not be any less content.
Young girls, though, yearn for married bliss
So ardently, that for my part
I cannot find it in my heart
To preach a doctrine such as this.

For my part, the biggest lessons here are don't marry the first man you see kneeling next to your bed, and for God's sake don't go on a summer holiday with your mother-in-law.

Other sleeping beauties
The tale on which Perrault based *Sleeping Beauty in the Wood* was published some sixty years previously by the Italian writer Giambattista Basile. *Sun, Moon and Talia* contains even more gruesome details, which Perrault tweaked and the Grimms left out altogether. In this earlier tale, the much longed-for daughter Talia is not cursed by a disgruntled fairy, but instead it is foretold by astrologers that she will fall foul of a 'splinter of flax'. Her father, a lord, thus bans flax from his house. But, needless to remark, a teenage Talia manages to find some outside the house, gets it stuck under her nail and 'dies'.

Her distraught father has her placed on a throne in his country mansion and leaves her there. One day, a king is out hunting. He enters the house and tries to rouse the seemingly sleeping girl to no effect. But rather than let a good opportunity pass, he has sex with her sleeping body/corpse. Date rape or necrophilia? You choose. Oh, and by the way, he's married.

While still unconscious, the girl gives birth to twins, a boy and a girl, who are thereafter tended to by benevolent fairies. One day the babies suck out the flax from under their sleeping mother's fingernail and she awakes. The charming, long-absent king returns for round two of sleeping sex but finds her awake and falls even more 'in love' with her.

His wife gets wind of the king's secret other family and orders a servant to kill and cook the children. But instead the servant hides them and substitutes lamb for their flesh, which the queen duly serves up to her husband. She then orders Talia to be brought to their palace to be burned but the king hears Talia's screams and comes running. The king and queen have a showdown – she tells him that she's uncovered his dirty little secret and that he has eaten his own children. She ends up in the fire for this. The servant is then able to produce the two children unharmed and the king is free to marry Talia. Presumably domestic bliss follows.

Basile's tale is likely to have been inspired by a

fourteenth-century French romance called *Perceforce*, which featured an episode in which the character Zellandine, who is given gifts at her birth by three goddesses, one of whom curses her to prick her finger on a spindle and fall into a deep sleep. She meets her love interest, Troilus, before the pricking incident – which occurs while he's away adventuring. He returns to find that she has fallen into her slumber and been hidden away in a tower with only one entrance – a high window. He gains access with the help of a spirit called Zephir, has sex with her sleeping body, impregnates her – and she later gives birth to a baby who sucks the offending flax out of her fingernail.

The Grimms' half-tale
The tale I knew from childhood was the Grimms' version, which, as previously mentioned, ends with the sleeping girl's awakening, and not a whiff of her flesh-eating mother-in-law or rival wife.

The Grimms' tale has some other basic differences. At the beginning of the story, a frog informs the queen that she will have her longed-for daughter before the year is out. And, at the feast held in her honour, twelve 'wise women' are invited. The king knows about the existence of a thirteenth but only has enough gold plates for twelve, so one is deliberately excluded. Big mistake. And the relevance of the number thirteen, long associated with superstitions around bad luck, is important to note here.

So the thirteenth 'wise woman' shows up, dishes out the spindle curse and disappears. But thankfully there is one gift left to be granted and so another wise woman can mitigate but not reverse the curse, as in the Perrault story. The lighter curse is again that the princess will sleep for a hundred years until awakened by a prince (note that the necessity of a kiss is again not mentioned). Also the new curse specifically states that this misadventure will befall the princess on her fifteenth birthday.

The king has all the spindles in the land burned, but of course the princess manages to find one out in an old tower when she's alone in the palace (why her parents elected to be absent on her fifteenth birthday is not elaborated on). She pricks her finger and collapses on to a conveniently placed bed. But she doesn't fall asleep alone. Everyone else – the king and queen included – does too. Even the flies on the walls are frozen in time.

And so again the briars grow all about the palace and a legend grows too about this strange place, its sleeping inhabitants and the beautiful princess. One hundred years to the day later, a prince is out hunting. He ventures to gain access to the palace, though countless men have tried and died doing so before. This is the one gruesome addition to the Grimm story – the briar hedge that surrounds the palace has claimed many lives: 'Indeed, they [other princes] could not pry themselves loose and died miserable deaths.' In his recent retelling of this tale, Philip Pullman adds that the hedge is littered with skeletons.

Luckily for this new prince, it's one hundred years to the day since the curse was enacted and so, when he approaches the briars, they turn into flowers and part easily for him. He walks through the palace, past all the sleeping bodies, and up to the tower where the princess lies in her coma. He falls instantly in love with her and plants a kiss on her lips, waking her up – and with her all the other inhabitants of the palace wake too. The prince and 'Briar Rose' are married and reportedly live happily ever after.

A kiss is not a prerequisite for waking up the not-quite-dead princesses, despite Walt Disney including it in his animated version of *Snow White and the Seven Dwarves* (1937) and thus enshrining it as a must-happen act in young imaginations thereafter. In the Grimms' *Snow White*, the apple that had kept the heroine in her coma was accidentally dislodged. And similarly Briar Rose would have awoken regardless, given that her hundred-years curse had just expired. FYI, girls – the princes and their magical wake-up kisses are window-dressing.

Along with *Sleeping Beauty*, other tales in which fairies or sorcerer's curses are the engine of the action include *The Frog King/Prince*, *Hans My Hedgehog*, *Ricky the Tuft*, *The Fairies*, *The Little Mermaid* and *Beauty and the Beast* to name but a few.

And in many of these the curse serves to take the central characters on a moral journey – usually to recognise inner beauty over objectionable surface appearance.

Celluloid Sleeping Beauties
The 'second half' of the Sleeping Beauty tale involving the cannibalistic mother-in-law/wife has been excised from screen versions of the story, and ballet versions, the most famous being by Pyotr Ilyich Tchaikovsky (1840–93). As have the necrophiliac tendencies of the 'hero'.

The German film *Dornröschen* (1955) follows the Grimm version closely, though it has the wicked thirteenth fairy, not a clueless old woman, coax the young princess to touch the spindle in the tower. And it also features a strange frog creature who shouts warnings at the princess during this sequence from the garden.

In the 1959 animated Disney version, the wicked fairy, now a witch called Maleficent, plays a lead antagonistic role throughout, which serves to make the prince a significantly more active character in the story. He must overcome the various obstacles she puts in his path and he even does battle with her in dragon form, before ultimately slaying her, to rescue his beloved. This telling also cements the idea created in *Snow White and the Seven Dwarves* (1937) that the 'true love's first kiss' is necessary to wake the sleeping princess, called Aurora. Like the early French version about Zellandine, the couple at least meet once in this film before the princess passes out.

Arch-enemy of the Disney film, fairy-tale scholar Jack Zipes describes the 1959 tale as 'one of the best examples of how he [Disney] and his huge staff of artists and musicians conventionalized the adaptation of fairy tales so that they became hollow and fluffy narratives and discredited original thinking...' Zipes goes on to say that Disney turned the tale into 'a banal adolescent love story in which a stereotypical nice-guy prince on a white horse rescues a pure blonde princess who awaits his blessed kiss while lying flat on her back.' (*The Enchanted Screen*, 2011).

In 2014, Disney released *Maleficent*, described as the 'untold story of Disney's most iconic villain'. In this film it is revealed that Maleficent, the evil sorceress from their 1959 *Sleeping Beauty*, wasn't actually that bad in her younger years, but was turned wicked as a consequence of a terrible betrayal. In this film, Angelina Jolie dons the iconic black antler-style headdress as the eponymous villain. Refreshingly, this tale focuses on the mother and daughter relationship that Maleficent and the Princess Aurora develop. And it also subverts the 'true love's first kiss' trope – which is terribly meta, given that Disney invented it in the first place.

BEAUTY AND THE BEAST

This story was first published as *La Belle et la Bête* in 1740 by French writer Gabrielle-Suzanne Barbot de Villeneuve who was heavily influenced by fairy-tale writers Madame d'Aulnoy and Charles Perrault. But the best-known version of the story was its hugely popular abridged retelling by Jeanne-Marie Le Prince de Beaumont in 1756, which was translated into English the following year.

Once again, a curse is the main engine for the action, but we are not told about it until the end of the tale. Instead, the story is a highly moral one about seeing beyond appearances, and that virtue and kindness are much more important qualities than physical beauty. Though luckily for the main character, her reward for learning this lesson is to have her fabulously wealthy but beastly paramour transformed into a dashing prince...

In de Beaumont's story, a rich merchant with six children, three sons and three daughters (all beautiful, but the youngest, Beauty, the prettiest of all), loses his fortune and the family end up living in a meagre farmhouse. One day, the father learns that some of his fortune may have survived on a ship and goes off to track it down. His two greedy daughters ask that he bring them back finery, while the sweet-natured Beauty asks for only a rose.

The merchant does not recover his fortune and on his way home gets lost in a forest, where he stumbles across

46

a fabulous palace kitted out with every luxury and plenty to eat and drink. Its owner is nowhere to be found. The merchant spends the night and, as he is leaving, he sees a rose in the garden, which he picks for his daughter. Only then does the palace's owner, a hideous 'beast', appear to chastise him and then threaten to kill him for daring to take the rose, which the beast considers the most precious object in the world. The merchant pleads for his life and the two strike a deal – one of the merchant's daughters must go willingly to the beast's palace, otherwise the merchant himself must return in three months to be killed.

The merchant returns home to see his children one final time before giving himself to the beast, but when Beauty learns of his fate she decides that she will go to the beast's palace herself and thus save her father.

Father and daughter go to the palace, where they meet the beast, and the following morning with much regret the father goes, leaving his daughter to her fate, which they presume will be death at the beast's hands. Specifically, that he will eat her. During her first day, she learns that the beast has only good intentions towards her and he appoints her mistress of his house. They dine together and he asks her to be his wife – she turns him down.

Then every night for three months they keep each other company and become friends. And every night the beast asks her to marry him, and every night she graciously declines. In a magic mirror she watches her father's plight at home, where he is sick with worry for her. The beast agrees that she can return to see her family for a week but with the caveat that if she doesn't return he will die of grief. He gives her a magic ring to use to travel between her father's house and his palace.

The next morning, she awakes in her father's house, causing quite a stir and bringing much joy to all but her newly married sisters who are sick with jealousy of her finery, gifted by the beast. They plot to get her to break her promise to the beast, hoping that it will have dire consequences for their sister. They feign distress when it comes time for her to leave and beg her to stay a week longer. She agrees, though she frets about the pain this will cause the beast whom she misses and wishes to see.

On her tenth night away, she has a dream that the beast is lying dying in the palace garden. She contemplates her own ingratitude at staying away and refusing to marry him because of his ugliness. She decides she must return to him the following day, placing the magic ring on her bedside table to effect her return to the beast's palace, where she wakes the following day.

She puts on her finest dress and waits for the beast to come that night. But he doesn't appear at his customary hour. Panic-stricken, she heads to the garden and finds him lying there close to death just as she had dreamt it. He tells her that when she failed to return he resolved to starve himself to death. She pleads with him not to die and says she will marry him. And then a magical transformation occurs – the beast becomes a handsome prince.

He tells her that he had been cursed by a wicked fairy to live as an ugly beast until a 'beautiful virgin' consented to marry him. Though why he was cursed in the first place is not elaborated upon. They return to the palace where Beauty's family are assembled along with a good fairy. The fairy curses her two conniving sisters to live as statues at the palace gate to witness their sister's happiness.

Beauty and her prince charming are transported to his kingdom where they marry.

THE FROG PRINCE

Sometimes known as *The Frog King* or *Iron Heinrich*, this tale was made popular by the Grimms.

Re-reading it as an adult, I was struck by the very young age of the princess character – and her petulant, violent nature. I'm pretty sure that the story I read in my fairy-tale treasury as a child was quite different to the Grimms' original.

Again, a prince has been cursed by a wicked fairy to live as an ugly creature, this time a frog. And his curse can only be lifted by a princess.

The age of the princess is not specified, but she is clearly a mere child, as the action starts with her playing with a golden ball by a well. She's throwing it up in the air and catching it, but when it slips from her 'little hand' and into the water she weeps bitterly for its loss. Doesn't sound like the behaviour of a sophisticated young lady to me…

So, the ball is in the water and up pops an ugly frog who strikes a deal with her to retrieve the ball. She agrees that she will let him be her companion and playmate, sit at the table with her and eat from her plate, drink from her cup and sleep on her bed with her at night. But the minute the princess has her ball, she runs off, leaving the frog behind her.

The next day, when she is at dinner with her father the king, the frog arrives looking for his due. When the king hears that his daughter has broken a promise, he chastises her and says she must honour her word to the frog. So she places him on the table next to her and lets him eat of her plate, then after the meal she has to carry him up to her room to sleep on her silken-sheeted bed. But when she gets to her room she can't face the idea of having a slimy frog spoil her nice clean bed, so she sets him on the floor instead. When he threatens to tell her father that she's breaking her promise again, she angrily picks him up and throws him against the wall with 'all her might'.

When the poor frog falls to the ground, he transforms into a prince with 'kind and beautiful eyes' – and this petulant little girl agrees to marry him. He sleeps in her room that night and the following day an elaborate coach shows up to conduct them to the prince's kingdom.

The coach is driven by 'Faithful Heinrich' who has had three iron bands wrapped around his heart to stop it bursting from grief for his master the prince's fate. Now that the prince is restored, the bands break apart from around Heinrich's heart – hence, the story's alternate title *Iron Heinrich*.

Now, you'll note that the whole petulant little girl dashing the frog against a wall is quite a different sentiment to the spell-breaking kiss the princess bestows in later retellings of the story. Again, we see the 'true love's first kiss' trope usurping the original. In the case of *The Frog King*, this infiltration occurred when the tale was translated into English. More often than not, Heinrich is also excluded from the end of the story. In Russian versions of the tale, the frog is an enchanted princess rather than a prince, whose bridegroom reluctantly marries her as a matter of honour.

HANS MY HEDGEHOG

Sometimes just wishing for something can be a dangerous activity. No fairies required. Such is the case in the bizarre tale *Hans My Hedgehog* recorded by the Brothers Grimm, a story that shares with *Beauty and the Beast* and *The Frog King* the theme of the importance of, and rewards for, keeping promises.

In this tale, a wealthy farmer wishes so hard for a child

that he declares he wouldn't mind even if it was born a hedgehog. After he has effectively cursed himself, his wife gives birth to a strange half-human, half-hedgehog baby. They call him Hans, and this strange child lives on some straw behind the stove for eight years, all the while being resented by his father.

One day, Hans asks his father to buy him some bagpipes at the market, and shortly thereafter asks him to have his rooster shod like a horse so that he might ride away on him, never to return. His father is only too happy to oblige.

So commences the second part of Hans the Hedgehog's strange life, herding donkeys and pigs in the forest and playing bagpipes in a tree with his rooster by his side.

Then the day comes where a king gets lost in the forest on his way home. Upon hearing Hans bagpiping, the king seeks him out for directions. Hans helps him on the condition that the king gives him the first thing he sees when he returns to his kingdom. The king hastily agrees – but with little intention of honouring his promise. It turns out that the first thing he sees upon his return is his daughter.

Then another king gets lost in the forest and as before asks Hans for directions, agreeing to give him the first thing he sees when he returns home. Again it turns out to be his daughter.

The day comes for Hans to collect his goods from the

kings. He goes to the first palace and is greeted by guards instructed to keep him out at all costs. Hans flies over them on his rooster and the king is forced to capitulate and his daughter leaves with the hedgehog man. On the road, however, Hans turns on his bride-to-be, makes her strip off all her clothes and pricks her with his quills until she is bloody from head to foot, then sends her home in shame as punishment for her and her father's deceit.

Hans then makes his way to the second palace where he is reluctantly welcomed, but the king and his daughter do not try any tricks to get out of their deal with him, and instead honour their promises. Hans and the princess are married and on their wedding night Hans asks the king's guards to help him – he will take off his hedgehog skin and they must burn it on the fire. They agree, and the skin is burned, but so is Hans. However, after a little balm is applied to his burns, he is transformed into a handsome young man, much to the princess's delight, and the king bequeaths his kingdom to him. Hans returns to see his father who is happy to receive him in human form and ultimately goes off to live with the royal couple in their palace.

THE FAIRIES

Also known as *Diamonds and Toads*, this story serves as a cautionary tale to children about being kind to their elders, especially old fairies. In the tale, there is a widow with two daughters, one kind, one nasty. In true fairy-tale fashion, the mother loves the nasty daughter best and treats the kind girl like a servant. One day, the kind daughter is sent to fetch water and meets a poor old woman who asks her for a drink. Of course the kind girl obliges and in return the old woman gives her a special gift that henceforth every time she speaks a flower or a precious gem will come from her mouth.

When she gets home and apologises to her haughty mother for taking so long, roses, pearls and diamonds pour forth from her mouth. When she then explains to her mother how she came by this strange talent, yet more diamonds pour forth.

Needless to say, the mother wants her other daughter to attain this power and sends her to fetch water. This nasty sloven, however, has never fetched a drop of water in her privileged life, but after some cajoling agrees to go. When she encounters the thirsty fairy, now dressed splendidly, she cannot help but be nasty to her and tells her to drink straight from the stream. In return, she is cursed so that every time she speaks a toad or a viper will issue forth from her mouth.

She returns to a horrified mother who instantly blames her kindly daughter for this misadventure and threatens to beat her, sending the poor girl fleeing into the forest. There she encounters a handsome prince who is instantly taken with her beauty – and when she speaks and he discovers her gift to bring forth riches, he whisks her off to his palace to marry her double quick.

As for her accursed sister, she becomes so hateful that her mother casts her out and she is left to wander from place to place. Nobody wants anything to do with her and so she is condemned to die alone in the forest.

A Basile tale is again thought to be the inspiration for this Perrault story. In his *Le Doie Pizzele* (*The Two Cakes*, 1634–36), two cousins, one good, one bad, encounter a hunchbacked lady who asks for food. The good girl gives her a whole cake she had put by for her own meal and is gifted so that flowers will issue forth from her mouth and jewels from her hair. When the bad cousin is tasked to follow suit, she eats her cake in front of the begging lady and is cursed so that foam will come from her mouth and toads from her hair.

Once again, the good girl who did right by the fairy gets the prince.

CHAPTER 2

SEX EDUCATION: CHASTITY, CHILD MARRIAGE AND A LITTLE INCEST

'Deeper meaning resides in the fairy tales told to me in my childhood than in the truth that is taught by life.'

– Friedrich von Schiller, poet, playwright and philosopher

Children are like little sponges – daily absorbing huge amounts of information that goes on to shape their self-perceptions and world views. The part played by the stories and rhymes we encounter in our formative years cannot be underestimated. And recently, modern parents have started questioning the lessons certain tales teach their little boys and girls about love and finding a partner… and what happens next once they do.

Many of what we now call nursery rhymes had a very adult audience when they were first in circulation and it shows – so many of them are riddled with innuendo and not-so-hidden meanings about human sexual relations. In this chapter, we'll unpick the messages of some of our best-loved rhymes and fairy tales – and the dark, sexual undercurrent that runs through so many of them. And if you think they're a little racy, wait until you hear the stories behind the stories. Prepare yourself for rhymes about prostitution and chastity belts, and tales of child molestation, incest and necrophilia. And that's just for starters…

PART I: NURSERY RHYMES

HIGGELDY, PIGGELDY, MY BLACK HEN

Higgeldy, piggeldy, my black hen
She lays eggs for gentlemen,
Sometimes nine and sometimes ten;
Gentlemen come every day
To see what my black hen has laid.

Little is known about the origin of this rhyme, first published in 1853. However, it wasn't too much of a leap for folklorists to link the rhyme to prostitution. And when you think of it in those terms, and imagine the narrator as a pimp or brothel madame, it's about as subtle as a kick in the face. There's an alternate version, in which eggs aren't specifically mentioned, and is all the more transparent in meaning for this omission…

> Hickety, pickety, my black hen
> She lays for gentlemen;
> Gentlemen come every day,
> To see what my black hen doth lay.
> Sometimes nine and sometimes ten,
> Hickety, pickety, my black hen.

A similar rhyme published in 1899 about a certain *Little Blue Betty* drops any pretence of subtlety:

> Little Blue Betty, she lived in a den,
> She sold good ale to gentlemen.
> Gentlemen came every day,
> And little Blue Betty she skipped away.
> She hopped upstairs to make her bed,
> But tumbled down and broke her head.

This Betty should not be confused with the other popular *Little Betty Blue*, who does nothing more exciting than lose a shoe:

> Little Betty Blue
> Lost her holiday shoe;

What shall little Betty do?
Give her another
To match the other
And then she'll walk upon two.

LAVENDER'S BLUE

Lavender's blue, dilly dilly, lavender's green,
When I am king, dilly, dilly, you shall be queen.
Who told you so, dilly, dilly, who told you so?
'Twas my own heart, dilly, dilly, that told me so.

Call up your men, dilly, dilly, set them to work
Some to the plough, dilly, dilly, some to the fork,
Some to make hay, dilly, dilly, some to cut corn,
While you and I, dilly, dilly, keep ourselves warm.

Lavender's green, dilly, dilly, Lavender's blue,
If you love me, dilly, dilly, I will love you.
Let the birds sing, dilly, dilly, and the lambs play;
We shall be safe, dilly, dilly, out of harm's way.

I love to dance, dilly, dilly, I love to sing;
When I am queen, dilly, dilly, you'll be my king.
Who told me so, dilly, dilly, who told me so?
I told myself, dilly, dilly, I told me so.

Lavender's Blue first appeared in print in the 1670s. In keeping with the appropriately 'blue' theme, this sweet-sounding song-cum-nursery rhyme is the better-known and sanitised version of an older rhyme *Lavender's Green*, whose words and intentions are a lot more direct, and tellingly used the word 'diddle' in place of 'dilly'. 'Diddle' frequently cropped up as a refrain in bawdy songs and is slang for intercourse and masturbation, though this is probably not its intended use here and certainly should not be applied to the rhyme *Hey Diddle Diddle!*

Here's the first verse of the older rhyme:

Lavender's green, diddle, diddle,
Lavender's blue,
You must love me, diddle, diddle,
'Cause I love you,
I heard one say, diddle, diddle,
Since I came hither,
That you and I, diddle, diddle,
Must lie together.

PETER, PETER, PUMPKIN EATER

Peter, Peter, pumpkin eater,
Had a wife and couldn't keep her;
He put her in a pumpkin shell
And there he kept her very well.

61

This rhyme originated in the USA, the home of the pumpkin, and first appeared in print in 1825. It's thought that Peter's wife was unfaithful to him and was therefore imprisoned in a 'pumpkin shell'. It has also been suggested that this could mean a chastity belt.

It appears to be based on an older British rhyme featuring some casual domestic violence:

> Eeper Weeper, chimney sweeper,
> Had a wife but couldn't keep her.
> Had another, didn't love her,
> Up the chimney he did shove her.

Which in turn comes from an older Scottish version (first published in 1868):

> Peter, my neeper,
> Had a wife,
> And he couidna' keep her,
> He pat her i' the wa',
> And lat a' the mice eat her.

Our Peter, the pumpkin eater, gets a second chance at love though, in the optional second verse:

> Peter, Peter pumpkin eater,
> Had another and didn't love her;

Peter learned to read and spell,
And then he loved her very well.

But back to the chastity belt...

Usually made of metal with a locking device, wearing one of these long term would have caused the wearer all manner of problems including abrasive wounds, infections resulting therefrom, potential sepsis and even death. Chastity belts (and their male equivalents) would have been used in fifteenth to the eighteenth centuries.

PART II: FAIRY TALES

A girl's purity and virginity are prized possessions in the fairy-tale world – as historically they have been in the 'real' world too.

Little Red Riding Hood is perhaps the most famous cautionary tale for girls, the metaphoric wolf representing the worst in men. In this section, we'll encounter lots of these wolves – some in their furry disguises, but others presented as kings and even fathers whose sexual appetites are dubious in the extreme...

LITTLE RED RIDING HOOD

Little Red Riding Hood serves as a warning to young girls about the dangers posed by men (represented by the wolf) and the importance of preserving their virginity. This is spelled out by Perrault in the heavy-handed moral at the end of his 1697 version, the first in print. Perrault places the responsibility of protecting their honour firmly at the door of little girls, and his tale tells them what their fate will be if they don't – a lesson that was softened and changed in subsequent versions of the story…

> Young children, as this tale will show,
> And mainly pretty girls with charm,
> Do wrong and often come to harm
> In letting those they do not know
> Stay talking to them when they meet.
> And if they don't do as they ought,
> It's no surprise that some are caught
> By wolves who take them off to eat.
> I call them wolves, but you will find
> That some are not the savage kind,
> Not howling, ravening or raging;
> Their manners seem, instead, engaging;
> They're softly spoken and discreet.
> Young ladies whom they talk to on the street
> They follow to their homes and through the hall,
> And upstairs to their rooms; when they're there
> They're not as friendly as they might appear:
> These are the most dangerous wolves of all.

According to writer Catherine Orenstein, the expression 'to see the wolf', meaning to lose one's virginity, passed into the vernacular in France following the publication of Perrault's tale. However, the best-known version of the story is the sanitised offering from the Brothers Grimm (published as *Rotkäppchen*, 1812). In this story, a much-loved little girl, known as Little Red Cap because of the velvet hat she wears, is tasked by her mother with visiting her ailing grandmother on the far side of the forest. She is given cake and wine to help nurse her grandmother back to health, and a stern warning from her mother not to stray from the path on her way through the woods. But Little Red Cap is a naive, trusting little girl, and when she meets a friendly seeming wolf she tells him of her mission to see her grandmother and is easily distracted by him when he draws her attention to the pretty flowers all around.

As she picks posies, the wolf heads off to her grand-mother's house, gains entrance by pretending to be Little Red Cap, eats the old woman, dons her clothes and lies in wait in the bed for the little girl to come along. When she arrives, she remarks how big her grandmother's ears, hands and mouth are, and she is eaten too.

The sated wolf returns to the bed and falls into a deep sleep, so much so that his loud snores draw the attention of a passing hunter. Quickly surmising that the wolf has eaten the grandmother, and that she may be salvageable from the beast's stomach (this is the fairy-tale world, where wolves swallow old women whole), the hunter sets about cutting open the wolf's stomach, which does not wake the wolf, and retrieves both Little Red Cap and her grandmother unscathed. They then fill the wolf's open belly with stones and stitch him back up. He awakes and tries to flee the scene but the stones weigh him down and kill him.

The end of this story is nearly identical to that of *The Wolf and the Seven Young Kids*, which is thought to be an older tale, and so the Grimms (or those who told them their version of the tale) may have borrowed it directly to give Little Red Cap the obligatory 'happy ever after'. In that story, a mother goat leaves her seven kids at home while she goes to fetch food, telling them not to open their door to anyone, especially not the Big Bad Wolf.

The aforementioned evil beast arrives at the door shortly thereafter, pretending to be their mother, but his gruff voice gives him away. Unsuccessful in getting at the kids, the wolf tries again later, this time having eaten chalk to make his voice softer. He nearly has the little goats fooled but they spot his big black paw on the windowsill and again he is sent away hungry. This time, the wolf gets some dough and flour, covers his paw and again with his softer voice begs admittance of the seven kids. When he shows them his white paw, they are convinced and let him in – where he eats them whole, one after the other. The mother goat returns to find her house trashed and her kids missing, except one who escaped by hiding in the clock case. Reunited, the two go into the forest and find the bulging, overfed wolf asleep under a tree. Seeing something move in his stomach, they fetch a scissors, needle and thread and set about cutting him open, rescuing the six kids. They fill his belly with stones and stitch him up again, all while the wolf sleeps on.

The wolf awakes with a mighty thirst and struggles to the nearest well. As he leans in to drink, the weight of the stones pulls him into the well, to the great delight of the goats who dance and sing in celebration at his death by drowning.

The Grimms also wrote an alternative version-cum-sequel to *Little Red Cap* in which the girl is on her way to her grandmother's once more, but this time, when she encounters a smooth-talking wolf, she is not distracted but instead heads straight to the house. There Little Red and her grandmother conspire to trick the wolf, who, after failing to gain entrance, has climbed on the roof. They fill a trough with water and lure him into falling into it with the smell of cooking sausages. He drowns.

In Perrault's earlier version, published in 1697, the wolf tricks Little Red as before, gets to her grandmother's house before her and devours the old woman. But, when the girl arrives and his identity is revealed, the wolf commands her to undress and get into bed with him. She obeys –

and is eaten. And that's the end of the tale. There's no huntsman, no redemption, only punishment for a little girl, foolish enough to be tricked and led astray by a wolf, taking off her clothes and climbing into bed with him.

Before she dies, she goes through the classic slow realisation that her grandmother has undergone a strange transformation:

> 'Oh, Grandmama, what long arms you have!'
>   'All the better to hug you with, my dear.'
> 'Oh, Grandmama, what long legs you have!'
>   'All the better for running with, my dear.'
> 'Oh, Grandmama, what big ears you have!'
>   'All the better to hear you with, my dear.'
> 'Oh, Grandmama, what big eyes you have!'
>   'All the better to see you with, my dear.'
> 'Oh, Grandmama, what great big teeth you have!'
> 'And they are all the better to EAT YOU WITH!'

Earlier versions

The earliest known version of the tale is an eleventh-century poem from Belgium that tells of a girl who wears a red baptism tunic, goes a-wandering and encounters a wolf.

A version from Italy/Austria published by Christian Schneller in 1867 called *Little Red Hat* swaps the wolf for an ogre. In this story, originating from a fourteenth-century folk tale, the ogre dispatches the grandmother in a grisly fashion, tying her intestines on to the door in place of the latch string and taking some blood, along with her teeth and jaws and stashing them in a cupboard.

When Little Red Hat gets to the house, she remarks to the ogre/grandmother how soft the latch string is, to which the ogre replies, 'Just pull and keep quiet. It is your grandmother's intestine!' When Little Red Hat queries the latter half of the sentence the ogre corrects himself: 'Just pull and keep quiet!'

The little girl says she's hungry and the ogre/grandmother directs her to the cupboard to eat. The little girl duly starts eating the teeth, thinking they're rice grains, and complains about their hardness. 'Eat and keep quiet. They are your grandmother's teeth!' she's told, and again, when she queries this, the ogre repeats just the first part of the sentence. The same happens with the jaws and the blood.

The girl next says she's tired, at which point the ogre invites her into bed – and there she notes how hairy her grandmother is, to be told, 'That comes with age.' When she comments on the length of her grandmother's legs, hands and ears, she's told it's from walking, working and listening, respectively. And when Little Red finally says, 'Grandmother, you have such a big mouth,' she's told, 'That comes from eating children!' And so Little Red is gobbled up.

Marie-Louise Tenèze and Paul Delarue include a cannibalistic, and overtly sexual, version of the Red Riding Hood tale, sometimes known as *The Grandmother* in their catalogue *Le conte populaire français* (1957). In this version of the folk tale, the gift for Little Red's grandmother is not wine and cake but milk and a bun. The wolf is a werewolf who tells the girl to take the 'needles' path, while he takes the 'pins'. Following his instructions, she picks up needles all the way to her grandmother's house. The wolf, having arrived there long before, has already dispatched the grandmother in a gruesome fashion – eating her, while keeping some of her flesh and blood in reserve. When Little Red arrives, the wolf tells her to put her milk and bun aside and instead to eat the 'meat' and drink the 'wine' there – thus cannibalising her poor old granny. The werewolf then tells her to get undressed and get into bed with him. Further, she is told to burn her clothes – as she will not need them again. In bed, she comments on the wolf's hairiness, his claws, ears and ultimately his mouth as per the usual story.

Before meeting her fate, Little Red says she has to relieve herself. Despite being told to do it in the bed, she manages to get out but the werewolf attaches a string of wool to her to keep track of her outside. When she gets outside, however, she attaches the string to a cherry tree and runs off. The werewolf gives chase, but she makes it home before he can catch her, presumably stark naked.

Little Red Riding Hood revisited

In her 1979 short story 'The Company of Wolves' from her book *The Bloody Chamber*, Angela Carter draws together elements from across these different versions to weave her own tale, which acts as a metaphor for a young girl's sexual awakening.

Unlike the Little Red of the Grimms and Perrault, whom Jack Zipes describes as 'a wimp' whose stupidity makes her 'complicit in her own rape/violation and death' or who 'needs the help of a hunter to free her...' (*The Irresistible Fairy Tale*, 2012), Carter's Little Red is a clever girl, well used to the dangers of the forest, and carries a carving knife for 'children do not stay young for long in this savage country'.

But when this girl on the brink of womanhood meets a handsome young huntsman she cannot resist his manly charms. When it is revealed that he is a werewolf and violently dispatches her grandmother, Little Red isn't afraid, she accepts her fate and almost happily undresses, before burning her clothes on the fire as the werewolf bids her – and, it is intimated, the two become lovers. In Neil Jordan's 1984 film adaptation of Carter's story, Little Red is herself transformed into a wolf, joining the pack in the forest.

In another Carter tale in the same collection, 'The Werewolf', a brave girl, not in a red cloak but in a 'scabby coat of sheepskin', gets the better of an attacking wolf with her knife and cuts off its forepaw. She takes the paw with her to her grandmother's house but finds her grandmother deathly sick in her bed.

When she takes out her handkerchief to make a cold compress for the old woman, the paw drops to the ground, except that it isn't a paw – it has turned into a hand, and an old one at that, with a wedding ring and a familiar wart on one of its fingers. Drawing back the bedclothes, the girl discovers that her grandmother's hand is missing, and that the bloodied stump that remains is already festering. The girl's cries bring the neighbours who identify the wart as a 'witch's nipple' and drive the old woman out into the snow and stone her to death. The girl moves into her grandmother's house and prospers.

Carter captures conditions as they might have been in the wild places that these tales were first told – places where life was brutal and short, food scarce and superstition rampant.

Little Red Riding Hood on screen

Little Red Riding Hood has inspired many interesting adaptations with sexuality at the centre, my own favourite being Jordan and Carter's The Company of Wolves (1984). Scouring the back catalogue of films and animations of the story in his book The Enchanted Screen (2011), Jack Zipes notes that Carter's story and Jordan's film 'shifted the literary and filmic discourse about the character and dilemma of Little Red Riding Hood from that of passive victim to a young woman, curious and confident, unafraid to fulfil her own desire'.

The 1996 film *Freeway*, starring Reese Witherspoon as Vanessa (Little Red) and Kiefer Sutherland as Bob Wolverton (the Wolf), shows just how profound the shift in the characterisation of the girl in red could be. Vanessa is a poor white-trash girl living in southern California with her prostitute mother and crack-addict stepfather. When her parents are arrested, Vanessa decides to head north to visit a grandmother she's never met to avoid being placed in a foster home.

She starts this journey with a gun from her gangster boyfriend and a car stolen from a social worker, but she doesn't get too far as the car breaks down on the freeway. Unfortunately for Vanessa, the knight in shining armour who comes to her assistance is Bob Wolverton, a serial killer operating up and down the freeway, the modern-day equivalent of the wild woods. Vanessa, however, is no passive victim, and manages to get the better of Bob, shooting him in the head and leaving him for dead.

It's not long before the police catch up with Vanessa and she finds herself in a juvenile detention centre. It transpires that Wolverton survived the shooting, though disfigured and disabled, and is hell bent on revenge through the courts system.

Vanessa escapes detention and begins her journey to her grandmother's house again. However, Wolverton is on the same mission, and gets there before Vanessa and kills the grandmother. At the end of the film, the two have a final showdown in which Vanessa beats her aggressor to death.

The film uses the framework of the *Little Red Riding Hood* story to attack various social and cultural ills in modern America – not least its love of violence and the poor state of its welfare, judicial and penal systems.

In *Hard Candy* (2005), starring Ellen Page and Patrick Wilson, fourteen-year-old Hailey meets thirty-two-year-old Jeff online and ends up going back to his house. But, rather than becoming a paedophile's victim, Hailey is a self-styled vigilante who has been stalking her prey online and intends to make him pay for his sick crimes – including conducting a castration operation and forcing him to hang himself. In an interesting reversal of the places used in the early stories, at the end of the film Hailey escapes from the ultra-modern world of the paedophile's house back into the woods.

The 2004 film *The Woodsman* gives us the story from the 'wolf's' perspective. Kevin Bacon plays Walter, a child molester returning to his hometown in Philadelphia after twelve years in prison. We follow his attempts to start a new life, resist the old temptations, and keep his past in the past – despite being harassed by a local police sergeant who bewails the fact that there are no woodsmen like the one in *Little Red Riding Hood* in the real world. In this story, the woods are replaced with a park and Walter works in a lumberyard.

As he starts to slip back into his old ways, Walter finds himself in the park, talking to a red-jacketed, lonely girl who has gone there to bird-watch. When he learns that her father is abusing her, he stops himself hurting her and to vent his frustrations beats a fellow paedophile he has been observing to a bloody pulp.

Most recently at time of writing, we've had *Red Riding Hood*, the universally panned 2011 film starring Amanda Seyfried and a selection of brooding young men who look like they've just stepped off the set of *Twilight*, whose director also directed this film – so they probably did.

Dropping the 'little' from the title, this story's heroine is an older teen, Valerie, who is in love with a brooding young man Peter. Her parents want her to marry another brooding, but wealthier young man Henry. Just as Valerie and Peter are about to run away together, her sister is killed by a werewolf who has been inactive for years. All hell breaks loose and the young lovers find themselves at the centre of the pretty lousy action.

DONKEY SKIN

From paedophilia to incest, *Donkey Skin* is another tale made famous by Charles Perrault in his *Tales and Stories* of the Past with Morals (*Histoires ou Contes du Temps passé*) in 1697.

Given the theme of this story – a father who wants to marry his daughter – this tale didn't catch on in quite the same way as others of Perrault's, though the Grimms did produce their own version, very similar in substance to his. Is the tale's subsequent exclusion from standard story-books a good thing? We're taught about 'stranger danger' but most cases of molestation, rape and murder are perpetrated by someone well known to the victim. So perhaps this tale could have some useful educational value…

The story, told in verse, begins by describing the rule and attributes of a powerful king and his beautiful wife, who have but one child, a daughter. The king owns Donkey Ned, a miraculous beast who dispenses riches from his behind and is the chief source of the king's wealth.

All is well until the queen falls ill. On her deathbed, she makes her husband promise that he will remarry only if he finds a woman more lovely and more virtuous than her. Before she expires, he assures her he has no intention of ever seeking another wife, but his resolve doesn't last long. A few short months later, he's on the market again, but, intent on keeping his promise to his deceased wife, he searches in vain for a bride of high enough quality to surpass her. That is, until he notices that his own daughter fits the bill.

The king falls madly in love with her and insists that they must wed. His daughter is distraught and weeps both night and day. She seeks advice from her godmother, a fairy, who advises her not to say no to him outright, but to set tricky conditions for the union. First, she must demand a dress the colour of the heavens – working on the assumption that such an item could never be made and therefore the wedding will be postponed indefinitely. But the lustful father calls upon the best dressmakers in the land and the following day is able to deliver a wonderful, sky-coloured gown to his daughter.

The godmother then advises that the girl ask for another dress, this time the colour of the moon – but again the king delivers the goods. She then asks for a final dress the colour of the sun – and once again the ardent king delivers. Having failed to put off the marriage by more than a few days, the godmother's finally advises the girl to ask for the skin of Donkey Ned – hoping that the father would never consider killing this miraculous cash cow. But no, the father has Ned killed and his skin presented to his daughter. Now she only has one option: to flee. Dressed in the donkey's skin with a dirtied face, the princess runs away armed with a wand she can use to conjure a casket full of jewels and her three splendid gowns when she needs them.

And so begins the second half of the story. Reduced to the status of a half-animal drudge, the princess, henceforth known as 'Donkey Skin', finds work at a farmhouse. In exchange for cleaning up after the family and their pigs, she gets a corner of the kitchen to sleep in. Because of her strange appearance she is mocked and abused by the peasants she now lives among. On Sundays, she washes the grime off her face and secretly dons her fancy dresses in turn to remind herself of who she really is and help sustain her through the harsh week ahead.

On one of these weekends, the son of the ruling king of the region is in the village. Donkey Skin sees him and is immediately attracted to his 'prince's air'. Later, he is walking by the farmhouse and sees the flash of a dazzling dress within, as Donkey Skin is having her private weekly fashion show. He does not make himself known, but instead returns to the palace despondent with love. When he enquires about this radiant beauty living in such an unlikely place, he is told she's Donkey Skin and is mocked. He is sick and miserable and his concerned mother asks him what he desires to get well. He tells her he wants Donkey Skin to bake him a cake. When the queen makes her enquiries as to who this Donkey Skin is, she is told in no uncertain terms that she's a 'miserable slut! / A dirtier beast you'll not find anywhere / A proper slattern!'

But the queen decides to give her son what he wants and so Donkey Skin is tasked with baking him a cake. She makes him a delicious one, and while making it her gold ring, either by accident or intent, falls into the mixture. The prince is delighted to find it – and keeps it under his pillow. But still his health continues to decline.

His parents decide that he needs to marry to restore his health. The prince himself is none too keen on their scheme, but says he will obey on condition that he marries the girl whom the gold ring fits. This offer is open to all women, high and low born, and so they come from across the land to try the ring, but it fits no one. Some are driven to desperate measures to get their fingers slim enough for the dainty ring. One women scrapes the skin off hers as you would a carrot, another dips hers in acid.

Finally, when all fingers have been tried and only Donkey Skin remains untested – she is called upon. A crowd has gathered to watch: 'What can he mean?' 'Allow her here?' 'That filthy creature?' 'What a joke!' But of course the ring fits and Donkey Skin is brought before the king – and when she does she appears resplendent in her sun gown.

The wedding day is a grand affair and all the kings and queens around are invited, including Donkey Skin's own father, who we're told has managed to banish from his heart the 'criminal desire' he once had for his daughter. And so they are happily reunited and all ends well.

Perrault adds his customary moral at the tale's end, this time stating that:

> sufferings, however stern,
> Are preferable by far to doing wrong;
> And next, whatever trials life may send
> Virtue will always triumph in the end;
> Also that love deranged defies all sense:
> Against it, reason is poor defence.

Notably absent is any warning against amorous fathers.

An old story
Many tales of a wealthy and powerful king wanting to marry his daughter emerged in the eleventh to the thirteenth century. Usually the father wishes to procure a male heir through their union. The daughter refuses and is cast out of the kingdom and/or mutilated in some way. She then wanders the countryside and forests, before eventually finding herself in another kingdom, attracting the attention of another king, whom she marries. But her troubles don't end there. Through some misunderstanding or slander, she finds herself cast out of her new home for a time, until her husband realises the error of his ways, seeks her out and reconciles with her once more.

Stories of this nature are found throughout Europe – in the folklore of Italy, the Basque country, Portugal, Germany, France, Austria, Romania, Greece, Lithuania, Russia and Scotland. The Italian fairy-tale collectors Straparola and Basile both recorded stories on the theme, and the Grimms recorded *All Fur*, also known as *All Kinds of Fur* in the early nineteenth century. In each of these versions, the father's desire for his daughter is depicted as a shameful, unnatural thing.

In Straparola's *Doralice*, found in his collection *The Facetious Nights of Straparola* (1550–55), the king is bound by a promise to only marry the woman whom his wife's ring fits – and that just happens to be his daughter. When he makes this discovery, he is 'assailed by a strange and diabolical temptation' to marry her.

To escape this fate, the daughter, Doralice, takes a potion that puts her to sleep and is hidden in a clothes chest, which is taken to England. The chest ends up in the bedroom of a prince, who finds the girl and marries her. Her unhappy father seeks out Doralice and contrives to murder the two children she has had with the prince, framing her for the crime. Her husband orders her to be stripped and buried up to the chin in the earth. He also orders that she is to be fed so that she will stay alive longer to be eaten by worms. Nice guy.

Her wicked, incest-minded father returns to his own kingdom and brags of his deeds in England. Hearing what he has done, Doralice's loyal old nurse travels to England to plead her case. She is freed and her husband gathers an army to take his revenge upon his father-in-law.

Doralice's husband clearly has a predilection for torture, for, not content merely to kill his father-in-law, he captures him and brings him back to England where he is racked, then pulled at with red-hot pincers, before being quartered and fed to ravening dogs.

Subsequently, we are told that Doralice and her husband 'lived many years happily together, leaving at their death diverse children in their place'.

In his 1634 telling of the tale as *The She-Bear*, Basile shows the king promising his dying wife that he will not remarry but his eye almost immediately falls on their beautiful young daughter Preziosa. She turns down his proposal, at which point he commands her to marry him that very night.

Preziosa confides her dilemma to an old woman who gives her an enchanted piece of wood. She tells her to put it in her mouth and that when her father comes to her she'll transform into a she-bear. Preziosa duly performs this strange task, is transformed, frightens her father off and flees into the forest.

Still in her she-bear guise, she meets a prince in the forest and the two form a bond. One day, he sees her in her human form and falls madly in love with her. But he then becomes ill. To aid his recovery, he asks that the bear be brought to his room to cook for him, and with his mother's blessing he and the bear share a kiss. At this, the wood falls from Preziosa's mouth and she is transformed back to her beautiful self. They marry and there is no further mention of her father.

All Fur

The Brothers Grimm wrote several versions of *All Fur* or *All Kinds of Fur* between 1812 and 1857. The fundamentals of the story are quite similar to Perrault's *Donkey Skin* and pull in elements of the *Cinderella* story. Again, a dying queen bids that, if her husband remarries, his future wife must be as beautiful as her and have hair as golden as hers. Lo and behold, when their daughter grows up, she fits the bill perfectly and her father falls in love with her.

But this time at least, everyone is horrified by the king's intention to marry his own daughter. His counsellors advise him that 'God has forbidden a father to marry his daughter. Nothing good can come from such a sin, the kingdom will be brought to ruin.'

However, the king isn't listening and presses on with the business of trying to marry his daughter. Without an advising godmother as per Perrault, the princess attempts to buy time for herself by requesting three dresses of otherworldly beauty, capturing the sun, moon and stars, respectively. She also asks for a coat made up of the fur and skin of every kind of animal in the kingdom – a thousand different types.

When the king manages to deliver these unlikely gifts, she is forced to flee into the forest. There she is mistaken for some exotic species of animal and captured by the hunters of another king. She is recognised as at least part human and so is put to work in the palace kitchen as a skivvy, and christened as 'All Fur'. And so the story segues into a *Cinderella* story.

One night, there is a ball, which she gets permission to watch at a distance. But rather than passively watching she takes out her dress like the sun, which she has been hiding in a magic nutshell along with various other precious things, and attends the ball in all her former splendour. She dances with the king who is enchanted by her. After their dance, she disappears, donning her fur disguise and hiding her beautiful face behind a mask of dirt once more. She is ordered to prepare a soup for the king, and into it she drops her gold ring.

The king eats the soup, which he says is the best he's ever tasted, and finds the ring. He calls upon the chef to come and explain it – which he can't and has to admit that All Fur cooked the soup. She is called but keeps her identity a secret and denies knowledge of the ring. Months pass, and the king holds another ball. Again, the mysterious and beautiful princess appears and dances with the king.

Once again she disappears at the end of the night. And again All Fur is charged with making the king his night-time soup. This time she drops a precious little gold spinning wheel into the bowl. And then there's the obligatory third ball of revelation. This time, the king manages to slip the gold ring on to his mysterious partner's finger and ensures that their dance is a long one in the hope of keeping her with him.

Hastening back to the kitchen, All Fur doesn't have time to change and so throws her fur coat on over her dazzling dress. When she is summoned again to the king to explain the latest token in his soup – a gold reel – the king sees that the furry creature is wearing the gold ring, he pulls at her furs and reveals the stunning dress. The soot and ashes are wiped from her face and the two are married. Her father is not in attendance nor is he mentioned again.

Sapsorrow

The *Donkey Skin* story has not been as revisited and rebooted as other Perrault tales, but it has had a few notable adaptations. The high-kitsch *Peau d'*âne (*Donkey Skin*) from 1970 starring Catherine Deneuve almost makes light of the father's incestuous intentions towards his daughter. And she in turn feels bad for refusing him – she would likely capitulate to his wishes if it wasn't for her insistent fairy godmother.

The Grimms' version is brought closer yet to *Cinderella* in *Sapsorrow* (1988), one of the tales featured in Jim Henson's *The Storyteller* series. The story is made 'suitable' for a younger audience, by changing the incestuous marriage proposal from one of lust to one of compulsion. It is written in the laws of the land that the king *must* marry the woman his deceased wife's ring fits. And it is with great sadness that he discovers that woman is his daughter Sapsorrow.

Again, the daughter asks for three brilliant dresses to stall the wedding, but she does not request her weird coat; instead, she crafts this herself with the help of the woodland creatures that inhabit her room in the palace. Once her coat is finished, she flees the kingdom and ends up working as a drudge in the palace of a handsome prince. Again, there is the ball – but rather than the soup motif of the Grimms' story, this version goes straight to *Cinderella* – and has the beautiful mysterious princess lose her slipper at the third ball – kicking off a quest to find the one it fits for the prince to marry.

At the same time, the prince and Sapsorrow, in her weird creature guise, start an uneasy friendship – one in which he abuses her and she moralises at him.

Sapsorrow also has two 'ugly' sisters borrowed straight from *Cinderella* and played brilliantly by comedy duo Dawn French and Jennifer Saunders.

Jim Henson's The Storyteller

Often creepy and always highly imaginative, this late-1980s TV series featured John Hurt as the eponymous Storyteller, weaving tales by his fireside for the benefit of his companion dog. The stories were usually a combination of Grimms fairy tales and German, Celtic, Russian and Scandinavian folk tales. Watching the series again recently, I was struck by how sinister some of the tales were and how unlikely it is that such a series would be produced for today's children some quarter of a century on.

As well as *Sapsorrow*, a reimagining of *Donkey Skin* and *Cinderella*, the series featured retellings of *Hans My Hedgehog* (p51), *Fearnot*, based on the Grimms' *A Tale About the Boy Who Went Forth to Learn What Fear Was*, and *The Three Ravens*, which draws on the German folk tale *The Six Swans* told by the Grimms.

RAPUNZEL

The Grimms published two versions of the *Rapunzel* story – the first in 1812, which included direct references to sex and pregnancy, and a sanitised second version in 1857, which didn't.

The second story is now the 'official' version and tells of a husband and wife who after a long-time wishing finally conceive a child. The couple live next to a delectable vegetable garden owned by a sorceress. It can be viewed from their house, but is protected by a high wall. One day, the pregnant wife sees some delicious-looking 'rapunzel' lettuce growing in this garden and is overtaken by a profound craving for the food – so much so that she falls ill. Her husband, worried that she might die from her craving, climbs the wall into the sorceress's garden and steals some lettuce for his wife. She delightedly eats it, but the next day her craving for the lettuce is even worse.

And so her husband again scales the wall, but this time he is confronted by the angry sorceress. When he explains that his wife's craving for the lettuce was potentially fatal, the sorceress strikes a deal with him. He must hand over the child his wife is carrying to her – and she will raise it like a mother.

And so the child is born and the sorceress appears to claim her – and that's the last we hear of the parents. Twelve years go by and the girl grows beautiful. So beautiful that the sorceress decides to hide her away in a tower in the forest, accessible only by a window some twenty yards up. To gain access the sorceress says:

> Rapunzel, Rapunzel
> Let down your hair for me

And so she climbs up by way of a long rope of the girl's golden hair. Years pass by with solitary Rapunzel living in the tower, visited daily by the sorceress, whose name is Mother Gothel. One day, a passing prince hears Rapunzel's beautiful singing and is drawn to the tower, but seeing no way in, he goes home disappointed. He returns the next day, and the day after that and so forth, to hear the enchanting singing of the tower's unseen occupant. And one of these days he witnesses the sorceress arrive and gain access via the hair-rope.

He comes back the next evening, calls out to Rapunzel

to let down her hair and climbs up. Understandably, the girl is frightened when this stranger jumps in her window, not least because she's never seen a man before. But he puts her at ease and tells her how he has been drawn by her singing and shortly thereafter proposes marriage to her. She accepts, thinking he may treat her better than Mother Gothel currently does.

But then they are faced with a problem – how can Rapunzel exit the tower? She bids her fiancé to return each day with a skein of silk for her to weave a ladder so she can leave. And so the two begin a new regime – the sorceress visits Rapunzel by day, and the prince by night with the silk skein.

One day, Rapunzel accidentally blurts out to Mother Gothel that she is heavier than the prince, who comes in her window so easily. Disgusted by the revelation that Rapunzel has been entertaining male company, she cuts off her lustrous locks and banishes her to a desolate, faraway country where she lives miserably. On the same night as her banishment, the prince arrives at the tower as usual, and climbs up but is greeted not by Rapunzel but by the wicked Mother Gothel, who curses him and tells him that 'The cat has got her [Rapunzel], and it will also scratch out your eyes.' Distraught, the prince jumps from the window into some thorns, which pierce his eyes and blind him.

Thereafter, he wanders alone for many years in

misery, eating roots and berries, until he eventually ends up in the same desolate land as Rapunzel, who in the meantime has given birth to twins – a boy and a girl – conceived in the tower with the prince (who at this point in the story the Grimms start referring to as her 'husband'). Hearing her singing, the blind prince is drawn towards Rapunzel and the two are overjoyed to be reunited. She cries tears on to his eyes, which restores his sight and the two return with their children to the prince's kingdom to live out the remainder of their lives in married bliss.

Rapunzel's purity
The version related above is a toned-down version of the original 'racy' 1812 version by the Grimms in which the innocent Rapunzel does not blurt out that the witch is heavier than the prince, but gives away that she is pregnant by commenting that her clothes have got tighter. The naive girl is obviously unaware of her predicament, and when you consider that this prince has been visiting her nightly in secret it shows him in a rather opportunistic light. Indeed, during their final confrontation in the tower, the witch calls him 'evil one'. In the later version, the fact that Rapunzel is pregnant with twins when she is banished is revealed rather matter-of-factly and, as above, the prince is thereafter referred to as her 'husband', even though no marriage has taken place.

This story is a warning about the preservation of chastity and the dangers of pregnancy. For starters, the pregnancy of Rapunzel's mother leads to her dangerous cravings, which in turn put her husband's life in danger and then result in the loss of their much longed-for daughter. Then the witch decides to hide Rapunzel away when she is on the brink of adolescence – so her aim may be to protect her from male advances. When she is unsuccessful in this endeavour and a man discovers her prized girl and gets her pregnant, the cost is high. Rapunzel is banished and her twin babies bring her yet more misery in the desolate land they trudge together.

Rapunzel's older sister
The oldest published version of this story is *Petrosinella* by Giambattista Basile (1634). In this tale, a woman called Pascadozzia sees some delicious parsley in the garden of an ogress and must have it.

So, when the opportunity arises, she steals some (no husband required). And she continues to steal the parsley until the ogress finally catches her but spares her life in exchange for ownership of her soon-to-be-born child. The ogress doesn't immediately claim the little girl Petrosinella, meaning Parsley; instead, she waits till she is seven and she meets her in the street on her way to school. The ogress cryptically tells the little girl to remind her mother of her promise. This happens each day for a time and eventually the mother instructs her daughter that, the next time the ogress gives her this message to relay, she is to tell her to 'Take it'. And thus the next time they meet, the ogress takes little Parsley away – grabbing her by the hair and pulling her into the darkest part of the woods. There she installs her in a tower, with only a high window by way of entrance – which is accessed by climbing Parsley's hair.

One day, a passing prince catches sight of the by then beautiful Parsley in the tower and the two quickly become intimately acquainted. A local gossip becomes aware of the prince's nightly visits and informs the ogress – but the exchange is heard by Parsley who resolves to run away with her lover that very night. She climbs from the tower by a rope and the two dash off, with the ogress in hot pursuit. Parsley has three enchanted 'gallnuts', which she throws in turn at the ogress. The first becomes a dog and the second a lion – both of which the ogress overcomes. But the third gallnut she throws turns into a wolf, which gobbles up the ogress before she can defend herself. And so the lovers go off to the prince's kingdom and are married.

Rapunzel syndrome

Rapunzel syndrome is the name given to a medical condition in which the intestines are damaged as a consequence of *trichophagia* – that is, the compulsive eating of human hair. A hair ball forms in the stomach and its long 'tail' sits in the small bowel and/or in the right colon. It leads to bowel obstruction and may need to be treated surgically.

CHAPTER 3

HISTORY LESSONS: BLOODY ARISTOCRATS, ROTTEN ROYALS, POLITICS AND CLASS

'The purest embodiment of the human condition'
– Humpty Dumpty as described in Paul Auster's 1985 novel *City of Glass*

Winston Churchill said that history is written by the victors – but nursery rhymes and fairy tales certainly weren't. While fairy tales often unquestioningly reinforce power structures and focus on the toing and froing of fantastical kings, queens, princes and princesses, many also show these royals in a far from favourable light, giving a flavour of what the general population, the folk in folk tale, really thought of them.

Nursery rhymes are laced with political intrigue and

95

tell-tale signs of the rot at the heart of the class systems of Britain, where most originate. Royals regularly get roasted – and the same figures tend to crop up again and again – most notably Richard III, Henry VIII, his daughter 'Bloody' Mary I, as well as the various members of the unfortunate Stuart dynasty.

PART I: NURSERY RHYMES

HUMPTY DUMPTY

Humpty Dumpty sat on a wall,
Humpty Dumpty had a great fall.
All the king's horses and all the king's men
Couldn't put Humpty together again.

Though it sounds a little implausible, it is theorised that Humpty Dumpty was intended as Richard III, the much maligned late fifteenth-century monarch who was reputed to be hunchbacked, and whose bones were recently uncovered under a car park in Leicester. Those who proffer this theory suggest that the name 'Humpty' is a direct reference to Richard's humped back, with the rhyme telling the allegorical story of his downfall at the battle of Bosworth Field.

'Humpty dumpty' is recorded in the *Oxford English Dictionary* as being a drink of brandy and ale popular in the seventeenth century. In the eighteenth century, it came to mean a clumsy person. It does seem a little more plausible to think of this character as being either a bit tipsy or clumsy, or both – hence that messy fall. He crops up in similar rhymes found in other European countries (France, Germany, Sweden, Norway), adding to the unlikelihood of the Richard III theory.

Humpty Dumpty made his first appearance in print in 1797 and was originally to be read as a riddle, the answer being 'egg' – hence Humpty is portrayed as one, and not a hunchback. The 1797 version reads:

> Humpty Dumpty sat on a wall,
> Humpty Dumpty had a great fall.
> Four-score men and four-score more,
> Could not make Humpty Dumpty where he was before.

In 1842, another rather gruesome version was committed to print, the egg-riddle element seemingly already forgotten:

> Humpty Dumpty lay in a beck.
> With all his sinews around his neck;
> Forty doctors and forty wrights
> Couldn't put Humpty Dumpty to rights!

LITTLE JACK HORNER

Little Jack Horner sat in a corner,
Eating a Christmas pie;
He put in a thumb, and pulled out a plum,
And said what a good boy am I!

As unlikely as it seems, this rhyme has been linked with Henry VIII's sweeping changes to the church in England, land grabs and a dodgy deal involving deeds stashed in a pie – all of which date it from the first half of the sixteenth century.

When Henry fell out with the Roman Catholic Church over the matter of his divorce from Catherine of Aragon, he took the opportunity to dismantle the enter Catholic establishment in England, dissolving monasteries and seizing their lands. The very last one to go, of over eight hundred religious institutions, was the Benedictine Abbey in Glastonbury. Richard Whyting, the Abbot there, had been an ally of King Henry, siding with him over the Pope and accepting him as head of the Church of England. To preserve his Abbey, he tried to do a deal with Henry, sending his steward – Thomas Horner – to the king offering him the deeds of twelve manor houses in exchange for him keeping the Abbey. It is said that the deeds were concealed in the crust of a large pie.

Thomas Horner, the 'Jack' or knave of the rhyme,

reportedly had a rummage in the pie in transit and helped himself to the deed for Mells Manor – a 'plum' piece of property if ever there was one.

Henry would not be bribed – though he did seize the deeds – and Abbot Whyting ended up in the Tower of London and was subsequently tried and executed for treason.

Descendants of Thomas Horner say the deceit is a fantasy – and have documentation to prove that Horner bought the 'lordship' from King Henry.

HARK HARK THE DOGS DO BARK

Hark hark the dogs do bark
The beggars are coming to town
Some in rags and some in jags
And one in a velvet gown.

This rhyme is again linked to the so-called 'dissolution of the monasteries' by Henry VIII. It wasn't just monasteries that were dismantled – convents, friaries and priories were also targeted, with over eight hundred institutions in total being pilfered by the king. This meant a lot of homeless nuns, monks and priests wandering the highways of England in the 1530s – and captured in this verse.

The reference to 'jags' is useful for dating the verse

– this is a style of slit in a garment exposing a material of a different colour underneath, which was particularly popular during Tudor times.

Or the verse could also simply refer to travelling entertainers…

MARY, MARY, QUITE CONTRARY

Mary, Mary, quite contrary,
How does your garden grow?
With silver bells, and cockle shells,
And pretty maids all in a row.

This rhyme has been associated with both Mary, Queen of Scots (1542–87) and Mary I of England, aka Bloody Mary (1516–58). Appropriately, Bloody Mary's association is the more gruesome of the two origin stories. It is speculated that 'How does your garden grow?' is a reference to the fact that Mary had no heirs. Her 'contrariness' is associated with her attempts to roll back the changes to the Church made by her father Henry VIII and her brother Edward VI – to restore Catholicism to England.

Silver bells and cockle shells are symbols associated with Catholicism. But it's the interpretation of the last line that gives the shivers, as the 'Pretty maids all in a row' are speculated to be either Mary's miscarried babies or women she'd had executed – there were a lot of them –

including the sixteen-year-old Lady Jane Grey, who was unfortunate enough to be nominated to the throne over Mary by Henry VIII's son King Edward VI, and reigned for just nine days. Lady Jane was imprisoned in the Tower of London, convicted of high treason and beheaded alongside her young husband, Lord Guildford Dudley.

THREE BLIND MICE

Three blind mice, three blind mice,
See how they run, see how they run;
They all ran after the farmer's wife,
Who cut off their tails with a carving knife;
Did you ever see such a thing in your life,
As three blind mice?

Bloody Mary is also associated with this rhyme about the strange mutilation of disabled rodents. When her father Henry VIII divorced her mother Catherine of Aragon – Mary became 'illegitimate', losing her position as a princess. She is subsequently supposed to have been referred to as the 'Farmer's Wife'.

The 'three blind mice' who all ran after the farmer's wife are meant to be three bishops loyal to Henry – Hugh Latimer, Nicholas Ridley and Thomas Cranmer, the Archbishop of Canterbury. These men were instrumental in dismantling Catholicism in England.

Henry died, leaving the throne to his sickly teenage son Edward who expired six years after him – passing the throne to Mary (once she'd dispatched pretender to the throne Lady Jane Grey, that is). When Catholic Mary was in charge, it was payback time for the three bishops. They were tortured and burned at the stake in Oxford in front of a crowd of disbelieving onlookers. It has been speculated that their 'blindness' may refer to their switch from Catholicism to Protestantism.

A very different version of the verse first appeared in print around 1609 in a collection of popular songs and verses compiled by Thomas Ravenscroft. It reads:

Three Blinde Mice,
Three Blinde Mice,
Dame Iulian,
Dame Iulian,
The Miller and his merry olde Wife,
She scrapte her tripe licke thou the knife.

THE LION AND THE UNICORN

The lion and the unicorn
Were fighting for the crown
The lion beat the unicorn
All around the town.

Some gave them white bread,
And some gave them brown;
Some gave them plum cake
And drummed them out of town.

These two royal beasts have a long history at odds with each other. The lion represents England and the unicorn Scotland. They briefly joined together when King James VI of Scotland became James I of England after Elizabeth I's death in 1603, uniting the Kingdoms under the Stuart dynasty. It didn't last long though, and the Stuarts were ultimately cast out of power – their various woes all memorialised, usually unkindly, in rhymes (more examples to follow).

The current royal coat of arms for the United Kingdom dates from this early seventeenth-century union, featuring the lion on the left and the unicorn on the right, where previously two lions had stood for England and two unicorns for Scotland on their respective coats of arms.

THERE WAS A CROOKED MAN

There was a crooked man, and he walked a crooked mile.
He found a crooked sixpence upon a crooked stile.
He bought a crooked cat, which caught a crooked mouse,
And they all lived together in a little crooked house.

This rhyme is reportedly about a certain Sir Alexander Leslie (1580–1661) a Scottish army general who played a significant role in the dethroning and execution of the next Stuart monarch, King Charles I. Leslie was something of a mercenary, fighting for the Dutch and Swiss armies too – and making a tidy income with it.

So rather than physically bent, crooked in this context means dishonest or disloyal.

When the National Covenant of 1683 was signed, denying that the king had a 'divine right' to the throne and binding the English and Scottish parliaments, Leslie marched his army from Edinburgh to the Scottish border (the crooked mile and the crooked stile, respectively), defeated the Royalist forces and effectively handed Charles over to the Parliamentarians who beheaded him outside the Banqueting House in Whitehall in front of a huge crowd (some of whom reportedly dipped their handkerchiefs in his blood as a sordid souvenir). The 'crooked house' was the alliance between the parliaments of Scotland and England.

The rhyme was first published in 1840, some 200 years after the events it supposedly cryptically records. Another, simpler explanation for the verse is that it's inspired by the town of Lavenham in Suffolk, whose old timber-framed houses lean at odd and opposing angles.

Illustrations accompanying the nursery rhyme in children's books since its publications feature a comically bent old man outside a lurching, leaning house and some-times attended by a similarly deformed cat and mouse, and no sign of a mercenary soldier or Stuart king…

GRAND OLD DUKE OF YORK

Oh, the grand old Duke of York,
He had ten thousand men;
He marched them up to the top of the hill,
And he marched them down again.

And when they were up, they were up,
And when they were down, they were down,
And when they were only half-way up,
They were neither up nor down.

This rollicking well-known tune is another with bloody, if disputed, origins. The oldest version of the song dates from 1642 as 'Old Tarlton's song' after the stage clown Richard Tarlton (1530–88) who made it famous:

The King of France with forty thousand men,
Came up a hill and so came downe againe

The version we know, however, didn't appear in print until 1913, though references to its use date from the 1890s.

Candidates for the Duke include Richard, the third Duke of York, who was effectively slaughtered when he went into battle without his reinforcements at the Battle of Wakefield in 1460. So, while he was the Duke of York, he most definitely had nothing close to ten thousand men in his army.

Then there's another beleaguered Stuart, King James II, Duke of York (1633–1701). He marched his army into battle with his Dutch son-in-law, William of Orange, at Salisbury Plain – but did not engage in the fight and instead retreated. So, though the Plain isn't a hill, his other actions fit the song.

Prince Frederick, Duke of York and second eldest son of George III, is the most popular of the three lead candidates. And there are two possible explanations as to why – one bloody, one not-so-bloody.

The bloody explanation is to do with the prince's career as field marshal during the French Revolutionary Wars (1792–1802). The prince was given the unenviable task of leading the British invasion of France – where he subsequently met with grim defeat when fighting along with Britain's ally armies at Tourcoing in 1794. Thousands of men were slaughtered. The prince himself survived and was recalled to England.

The not-so-bloody explanation is that, when the prince was having an elaborate temple folly constructed on top of a 200-foot hill at his estate at Allerton Castle near Harrogate, the workmen travelling up and down lugging materials could be seen for miles around.

GOOSEY, GOOSEY GANDER

Goosey, goosey gander,
Whither shall I wander?
Upstairs and downstairs
And in my lady's chamber.
There I met an old man
Who wouldn't say his prayers,
So I took him by his left leg
And threw him down the stairs.

This casually violent little number didn't start off including geriatric abuse; in fact, its first printed iteration in 1784 was a harmless nonsense rhyme:

Goose-a-goose-a gander,
Where shall I wander?
Up stairs and down stairs,
In my lady's chamber;
There you'll find a cup of sack
And a race of ginger.

But the more popular version we know today borrows its final section from a separate playground rhyme about crane flies, lacing it with sinister undertones of persecution. It's hypothesised that the rhyme in its current form is about Cromwell's army of 'roundheads' (possibly marching in goose-step) persecuting Catholics (known as left-footers – the left being associated with the devil). When read in this context, it does seem rather like a raid on a house taking place and a dissenting old man (possibly a priest) being manhandled…

LITTLE TOM TUCKER

Little Tom Tucker sings for his supper.
What shall we give him?
White bread and butter.
How shall he cut it without a knife?
How will he be married without a wife?

As well as capturing the political mood of certain eras and reigns, some nursery rhymes provide an insight, often bleak, into class systems and working conditions.

This verse is thought to be about an orphan, so poor he has to sing for his supper and doesn't even possess a knife. His low status also means he's unlikely to marry. 'Tommy Tucker' was a generic name commonly given to orphans in popular culture. The earliest version in print is from 1744.

SEE-SAW, MARGERY DAW

See-saw, Margery Daw,
Johnny shall have a new master;
He shall earn but a penny a day
Because he can't work any faster.

See-saw, Margery Daw,
Sold her bed and lay on straw;
Wasn't she a dirty slut
To sell her bed and lie in the dirt?

See-saw, Margery Daw,
The old hen flew over the malt house;
She counted her one by one,
Still she missed the little white one,
And this is it, this is it, this is it.

This song is associated with children playing on a see-saw, and is thought to have originally been sung by men sawing wood in pairs to help keep time. But it also has associations with child labour.

The first verse refers to the fate of 'Johnny' who will earn just a penny a day under his new master. It sounds like a taunt of Johnny's abilities ('because he can't work any faster'). Then Margery herself is forced to sell her bed and sleep on straw – and for this she is branded 'a dirty slut'. 'Slut' doesn't necessarily have a sexual connotation – but for a girl in these reduced circumstances the spectre of prostitution wouldn't be far away. In the final verse the 'malt house' may represent the workhouse – where destitute children would find themselves in the eighteenth and nineteenth centuries (the rhyme first appeared in print in 1765).

There's an overall air of cruelty to the whole thing – which it's all too easy to imagine being dished out to workhouse children. There's something especially taunting and menacing about that last line – 'And this is it, this is it, this is it.'

From 'dirty sluts' to 'dirty sows', the verse *I Am a Pretty Wench* from James Orchard Halliwell's *The Nursery Rhymes of England* (1842) provides another insight into the casually vicious terminology applied to women of the day:

> I am a pretty wench,
> And I come a great way hence,
> And sweethearts I can get none:
> But every dirty sow,
> Can get sweethearts enow,
> And I, pretty wench, can get never a one.

GIRLS AND BOYS, COME OUT TO PLAY

> Girls and boys, come out to play,
> The moon doth shine as bright as day;

Leave your supper, and leave your sleep,
And come with your playfellows into the street.
Come with a whoop, come with a call,
Come with a good will or not at all.
Up the ladder and down the wall,
A halfpenny roll will serve us all.
You find milk, and I'll find flour,
And we'll have a pudding in half an hour.

Another rhyme associated with child labour, this one is thought to illustrate the fact that working children would only have the opportunity to play at night. This rhyme was first published in 1708.

BAA, BAA, BLACK SHEEP

Baa, baa, black sheep,
Have you any wool?
Yes sir, yes sir,
Three bags full;
One for the master,
And one for the dame,
And one for the little boy
Who lives down the lane.

This song has long been associated with a thirteenth-century export tax on wool. This tax was in place for some 200 years, so the rhyme could have originated at any time during the thirteenth and fourteenth centuries. Wool was big business in medieval England, and English wool was in hot demand on mainland Europe – hence greedy overlords could easily raise extra money for their personal coffers by upping the tax on it.

The crusader king Edward I first imposed the tax to raise money for his military campaigns. The crown took the equivalent of a third of the value of each sack of wool. So the way the three bags are apportioned in the rhyme reflects how a third would go to the master (the king).

In the version found in *Mother Goose's Melody* (1765), the last line reads: 'And none for the little boy who cries in the lane' – and it is thought that would have been the standard final message until the later softening of the rhyme. This little boy can perhaps be seen as the shepherd – who gets little or nothing for his work caring for the sheep, relative to the greedy king.

The line 'yes sir, yes sir' sounds a little harried and grovelling – as if the 'sheep' is being asked about the wool by someone in a superior position.

Bleep, Bleep, Black Sheep
'Baa, Baa, Black Sheep' was among the first songs to ever be played by a computer. Back in 1951 at Manchester University, a gargantuan computer affectionately known

as 'Baby' (but officially a Ferranti Mark 1) played 'God Save the Queen', *Baa Baa Black Sheep* and 'In the Mood'!

POP GOES THE WEASEL

There are a number of variations of this verse, so I'll reproduce the best-known (and longest) version here:

Half a pound of tupenny rice,
Half a pound of treacle.
That's the way the money goes,
Pop goes the weasel.

Up and down the City Road,
In and out the Eagle.
That's the way the money goes,
Pop goes the weasel.

Every night when I go out,
The monkey's on the table.
Take a stick and knock it off,
Pop goes the weasel.

A penny for a ball of thread,
Another for a needle.
That's the way the money goes,
Pop goes the weasel.

This song has its origins in the extreme poverty of London's East End in the nineteenth century. 'Weasel and stoat' was cockney rhyming slang for 'coat' and the expression 'to pop' means to pawn. At its most basic, the song is about repeatedly running out of money and having to pawn a coat over and over to get by. Grim stuff.

First the singer's money goes on food. Then on drink – The Eagle was (and is) a pub on East London's City Road, and 'monkey' in the third verse may refer to a tankard of ale. The thread and needle of the last verse may refer to the profession of the singer and having just enough money to buy the tools of his trade (the part of London referred to in the song was known for its textile industry). Or perhaps the singer has just enough to fix the well-worn and often-pawned coat before selling it again…

The tune became a hugely popular dance in the music halls and theatres of mid-nineteenth-century England. And made its way across the Atlantic to enjoy similar success in America.

I grew up with the American version of the rhyme, which had little to do with poverty and a lot to do with nonsense and featured in chasing games. The opening lines were:

> All around the Mulberry Bush,
> The monkey chased the weasel.

The monkey stopped to pull up his sock, [or The
monkey stopped to scratch his nose]
Pop! Goes the weasel.

PART II: FAIRY TALES

So far, we've seen many fairy tales centred on royalty –
kings, queens, princes, princesses… and those who want
to either curry favour with or marry them. And, more
often than not, the station in life of these royals is a given
– born to, rather than earned – and not to be questioned.

But, in this section, we'll look at a selection of tales that
highlight the blinkered greed of monarchs, question the
legitimacy of their rule and their 'royal blood', and also
show the lows they can sink to in their pursuit of power
and wealth.

While older tales in the folk tradition tended not to
question power structures, the stories of Danish writer
Hans Christian Andersen (1805–75) are rife with satire
and social commentary. When he died, Andersen was
rated alongside Charles Dickens as the world's favourite
author. Like Dickens, he wrote not just about the high
and mighty, but also the marginalised and persecuted. In
his tales he sympathises with the poor (*The Little Match
Girl*), the disabled (*The Steadfast Tin Soldier*), the Jews (*The
Jewish Girl, Only a Fiddler*) and those outside of society who
had to live by their wits alone (*Little Claus and Big Claus, The*

Tinderbox). He also pokes fun at nobility in tales such as *The Emperor's New Clothes* and *The Princess and the Pea* – both of which we'll look at in more detail shortly.

But first, let's consider an older tale, which celebrates getting one over on rich royals with aplomb…

PUSS IN BOOTS

Flattery, trickery and threats – this con-artist cat is a political maneuverer of the highest calibre. Published in 1697 by Charles Perrault as *Le Maître Chat, ou le Chat Botté* (Master Cat, or The Booted Cat), the well-known title *Puss in Boots* is first found in an English translation by Robert Samber in 1729. Samber's tale was advertised as being 'very entertaining and instructive for children', though the nature of this instruction is perhaps a little dubious.

Perrault's Puss
There was once a miller who had three sons. Upon his death, he bequeaths his mill to his eldest son, his donkey to his middle son and his cat to his third son. Understandably, the third son feels somewhat hard done by and wonders how he is going to live with only a cat to his name. In fact, the only worth he can see in the cat is either as something to eat or something to wear – but neither will sustain him for long.

The cat, however, has other ideas and tells his master that if he'll provide him with a pair of boots and a bag he'll make sure he's provided for. Having witnessed the cat's cunning when it comes to hunting mice, the young master assents.

The cat uses the bag as a trap to lure rabbits and decides to present one of his catches to the king on behalf of his master, whom he claims is the 'Marquis of Carabas'. This becomes the cat's regular habit, bringing rabbits, partridges and other game as offerings to the king on behalf of his unwitting master.

We are not told what the young master is doing in the interim period to improve his lot, other than eating the game his cat brings home...

One day, the king and his daughter are passing through the area where the cat and his master live. Puss gets wind of this and tells his master he'll help him make his fortune and instructs him to go bathe in the river at a particular spot. His master obeys and the cat stashes his clothes. When the king's carriage goes by, the cat starts screaming for assistance, saying his young master is drowning. And then that his clothes have been stolen.

His master is rescued and dressed in finery from the king's carriage. He cuts a handsome figure and the king's daughter is immediately taken with him. The master plays the role of the marquis and joins the king and his daughter on their outing.

The cat runs ahead of their carriage to instruct various farm labourers dotted about that they are to tell the passing king that the land they work belongs to the Marquis of Carabas, and that if they don't they will be 'chopped up as fine as sausage meat'. The peasants duly obey and the king is impressed by the marquis' span of land.

Next the cat races to a grand castle owned by a particularly wealthy ogre. The cat challenges the ogre to demonstrate his ability to transform into different animals. First, the ogre transforms into a lion, then, at the cat's suggestion, a mouse. The second the ogre changes, the cat pounces on the mouse and eats it. His next trick is to pass off the ogre's castle as the residence of the Marquis of Carabas and get the king tipsy. He does both successfully, and when the king is feeling relaxed after a few glasses of wine he offers the marquis his daughter's hand in marriage.

The two marry that very day and the 'marquis' makes the cunning cat a lord, who never has to chase a mouse again, except to please himself.

The moral of the story
So, one wonders again what exactly this story is 'instructing' children about. In his trademark moral at the end, Perrault posits a double lesson for the young reader:

Although the benefits are great
For one who owns a large estate
Because he is his father's son,
Young men, when all is said and done,
Will find sharp wits and commonsense
Worth more than an inheritance.

If the son of a miller, in ten minutes or less,
Can take a girl's fancy, and make a princess
Look longingly at him, it proves an old truth:
That elegant clothes on a good-looking youth
Can play a distinctly significant part
In winning the love of a feminine heart.

The first is nice enough – that money isn't everything, and certainly not inherited rather than earned money. And the second is basically that 'clothes make the man'. The fact that the 'man' in this tale was effectively a passive presence who did everything a cat told him to is not alluded to!

As folklorists Iona and Peter Opie put it, 'the tale is unusual in that the hero little deserves his good fortune, that is if his poverty, his being a third child, and his unquestioning acceptance of the cat's sinful instructions, are not nowadays looked upon as virtues' (*The Classic Fairy Tales*, 1974).

George Cruikshank, illustrator of the books of Charles

Dickens, expressed shock that parents allowed children to read the story: 'As it stood the tale was a succession of successful falsehoods – a clever lesson in lying! – a system of imposture rewarded with the greatest worldly advantages.'

It is worth noting that Cruikshank and Dickens fell out over the increasing conservatism of the former.

The Grimms' version

The Grimms' *Der gestiefelte Kater* was first published in 1812 but was omitted from their next collection of tales in 1819 because of its French origin (Perrault's tale), which jarred with their mission to promote German folklore.

In their tale, the cat explains to his down-at-heel master that he wants the boots so that he can 'go out, mix with people, and help you before you know it'. In this tale, the fact that this cat can talk and walk upright is rightly seen as unusual by the general populace.

The king of this story has a strong taste for partridges but none of his hunters can catch any – so the cat sees his opportunity and starts hunting. He presents partridges to the king as an offering from his master 'the count'. But in this telling he is generously rewarded for this catch – the king allows him to take as much gold as he can manage from the treasury, a trick he repeats daily to his master's great delight.

The cat becomes a regular fixture at the palace and, one day, as he's warming himself by the fire in its kitchen, he overhears a coachman complaining that he has to take the king and his daughter the princess on a pleasure jaunt to the lake. Armed with this information, the cat gets his master to strip naked and take a swim in the lake while he stashes his clothes, and seeing the king's carriage approach starts to shout that his master 'the count' has been robbed. A servant is sent back to the palace to fetch clothes and the miller's son is adorned in kingly raiment and invited to join the royals in their carriage. Happily, the princess is quite taken by the handsome young man.

Next the cat dashes ahead and tells labourers he meets in the meadow, wheat field and forest to say that the land belongs to 'the count' or be killed. We're told that 'since he looked so unusual and walked in boots like a human being they were afraid of him' and did his bidding.

The land and the forest belong to a sorcerer, and it is to his magnificent palace that the cat goes next. There he uses a combination of flattery and dares to coerce the sorcerer into changing shape – first into an elephant, then into a lion and finally into a mouse which the cat duly catches and eats.

Meanwhile, the cat's roadside ruse is working and the king is impressed with the evident wealth of 'the count'. Seeing the palace seals the deal, and the count and the princess marry.

When the king passes away, the count is crowned as his successor and he appoints the cat his prime minister.

Before Perrault

Straparola and Basile wrote similar stories featuring the trope of the 'cat helper' in the mid-sixteenth and early seventeenth centuries respectively. In Straparola's *Lucky Costantino*, the third son of a poor woman inherits a female cat who turns out to be a fairy. The cat looks after him (including feeding and washing him) and brings tributes to the king as per Perrault and the Grimms. But, when the cat and her master pull their river drowning stunt, the cat tells the king that her master was bringing jewels to the palace as a gift but was attacked and robbed. In return for this, the king offers Costantino his daughter's hand in marriage. The next problem is where the newlyweds will live, but by good fortune the cat secures a castle in which the owner has just died. Later Costantino becomes king.

Basile's is a story about gratitude. In *Gagliuso*, a poor Neapolitan man leaves one son a sieve and the other a cat. The sieve is considered the better bequest. The cat is again female and helps her master by bringing offerings to the king to win his favour. The king asks to meet Gagliuso and the cat manages to get him some fine clothes and covers up his uncouth ways and ill-bred remarks at the palace. She also brags about her master's huge wealth and vast estates. The king sends his daughter and a retinue to investigate these claims. Again, the cat cajoles people along the way to say Gagliuso is their master. The fix is in and Gagliuso marries the princess and buys a country estate with the dowry he gets.

Delighted with his good fortune, Gagliuso expresses his profound gratitude to the cat for all her help, saying he'll give her an elaborate burial when she passes. However, the cat decides to test the sincerity of her master and fakes her own death – and finds that not only is Gagliuso not moved, he actually instructs his wife to throw the cat's body out the window.

The cat leaves for good – disgusted at Gagliuso's ingratitude, which is in stark contrast to later versions where the cat gets appointed a lord and even a prime minister.

THE EMPEROR'S NEW CLOTHES

Another tale that highlights how easily even royals can be fooled is this Hans Christian Andersen story of a vain monarch and his bumbling cronies. This searing satire uses the fairy-tale form to expose the sycophantic self-interest of those in power.

Andersen tells us of an emperor whose primary interest in life is clothes – so much so that he is not to be found sitting in council but in his wardrobe. One day, two strangers show up in the capital city, bragging about their otherworldly weaving skills. They claim that they can make a cloth so fantastic and fine that it is invisible to all who are unfit for the office they hold or are otherwise profoundly stupid.

The emperor buys this nonsense hook, line and sinker and commissions an outfit from them. He also believes that this wondrous fabric will help him weed out the incompetents in his realm.

Large sums of money are bestowed upon the weavers, along with delicate silks and gold threads – all of which they pocket and instead work on empty looms creating their magical cloth.

Anxious to know how work is progressing on his new suit but fearful of checking himself, lest he discover that he is either unfit to rule or just plain dense, the emperor decides to send a trusted old minister to inspect the cloth for him. So, the minister attends the weavers and, being unable to see anything in their looms, but unwilling to admit it, praises their fabulous work and promises to give it a hearty endorsement to the emperor. The weavers thank him and make sure to describe in detail the colour and design of the non-existent cloth to make the minister's lie a little easier to tell.

More time passes with the weavers hard at work on their empty looms and demanding yet more money and expensive materials. Again, the emperor wants a progress report and again is shy of going himself, so he sends another officer of his court – who must go through the charade of pretending to see the cloth for fear of being exposed as unfit and/or stupid.

Soon the whole city is abuzz with stories of this miracle

cloth and the emperor's planned parade to show off his suit made of it. The emperor's own anticipation gets the better of him and he visits the weavers with an entourage – all of them, himself included, pretend to see what isn't there on the looms. All gasp with delight and praise. The emperor, afraid of being exposed, proclaims the cloth magnificent, charming and excellent, and presents the impostors with a riband of an order of knighthood, making them 'Gentleman Weavers'.

The night before the emperor's parade, the weavers make a great show of staying up late to work on the suit. The next day, they present the finished article to the emperor, telling him that it is as light as a cobweb and gives one the impression of wearing nothing at all. They dress the emperor in his new mantle, which he pretends to admire in the mirror. Then the men tasked with carrying his train make a show of picking it up from the floor and carrying it after the emperor.

Out he goes into the street under a high canopy and crowds of his admirers all shout praise at the fineness of his outfit, each one afraid to give themselves away and be thought unfit and stupid by the other.

But then a little child proclaims: 'But the emperor has nothing at all on!' And his father adds his support, urging others to 'Listen to the voice of innocence.'

Soon all the crowd begin to chant that the emperor has nothing on – and though the great man himself also knows it – he continues his procession. And his train bearers continue to hold up his invisible train.

Backstory

This tale was first published in 1837 in the third and final instalment of Andersen's *Fairy Tales for Children*. The story goes that it was on its way to the printers when Andersen recalled it and added his now iconic ending with the innocent child pointing out the grown-ups' folly.

It is theorised that Andersen may have decided to do this after reading the story to a child and realising the added depth this tweak could bring. Or it could be that he decided to inject a bit of autobiographical detail.

In later life, Andersen recounted a tale about being brought to see King Frederick VI in procession, where he called out to his mother, 'Oh, he's nothing more than a human being!', to which his mother responded, 'Have you gone mad, child?'

The source for the story is a German translation of an early fourteenth-century Spanish story from a collection of cautionary tales called *Libro de los ejemplos*. In this older tale, cunning weavers trick a king into buying a suit of invisible cloth, which they claim cannot be seen by those who do not know who their fathers are. Therefore, men are unlikely to admit that they can't see the cloth and announce themselves as illegitimate. It's a sort of magical paternity test.

The Emperor's on-screen message…

While Andersen's tale exposes the hypocrisy and vanity of the ruling class, it does not give any insight into the society in which the story takes place, nor the aftermath of the emperor's naked parade. In the 1984 version of the tale from the US series *The Faerie Tale Theatre*, we see how the splendour of the court contrasts with the lives of the lower classes – dressed in rags and crippled by taxes to facilitate the lavish lives of the rich. The swindler weavers are more like Robin Hood figures: they steal from the rich (the emperor) and give to the poor via an innkeeper who looks set to lose her business because of the high taxes she must pay.

According to Jack Zipes, this telling 'shifts the focus to questions of government, social injustice, and reform – questions that were appropriate during the Reagan regime in America throughout the 1980s…' (*The Enchanted Screen*, 2011).

Disney revisited the emperor story in 2000 with *The Emperor's New Groove* described by Zipes as 'putrid and stale' with an 'offensive' plot.

The story bears little resemblance to Andersen's. The action centres on Kuzco, a selfish eighteen-year-old emperor of the Incan Empire. Spoiled and incredibly rich, Kuzco decides to give himself a birthday treat – building a huge summer palace 'Kuzcotopia' on the site of one of his subject's homes. The soon-to-be-homeless Pacha protests in vain. Meanwhile, enemies of the emperor, the witch Yzma and her dumb henchman Kronk, decide to poison the boy-emperor and seize control – except that, rather than poison, they give him a potion that turns him into a llama. The llama emperor encounters Pacha again – who ends up saving his life and helping him become human again. At the end, the emperor is humbled and, rather than build his ostentatious new palace, he builds a small cabin instead.

In terms of morals, this film does not compare favourably with its supposed source text. Zipes describes it as an ideological 'disaster', which 'displays South Americans in stereotypical forms and repeats the totalitarian message that almost all the Disney films have conveyed since their origin: the role of the peasants or little people is to help to reinstall kings, emperors, queens, princesses and other celebrities so that they can rule more graciously.'

THE PRINCESS AND THE PEA

This 1835 Hans Christian Andersen story has been read in a few ways. Some critics say that it serves to affirm the 'specialness' of royal blood – a notion that helps keep various monarchs in business to this day. Others that the demented bed test highlights the ludicrous notion that one is born royal or that there is such a thing as a 'real

princess'. To my mind, the latter has the stronger case –
as we shall see…

Once upon a time, there was a prince who wanted to
marry – but his wife would have to be a 'real' princess. He
searched high and low but he couldn't find a young lady
who qualified. 'There was always something about them
that was not as it should be.'

He returned home after his failed search and fell into
a sadness – wondering if he'd ever find this authentic
bride. One stormy night, there was a loud knocking
on the palace gate – a young lady, soaked to the bone,
had come to seek out the prince. She said that she was
a 'real' princess. Though the prince's mother, the queen,
thought otherwise. To test this wet and unwitting girl, the
queen laid a pea on the base of a bed, then piled twenty
mattresses and twenty eiderdowns on top and announced
that this would be the princess's bed for the night.

The following morning, the queen asked the girl how
she had slept – very badly, she was told. The princess
complained that she slept on something hard and that
she was black and blue from it.

The queen was delighted by this news, as extra
sensitivity is meant to be a hallmark trait of a real princess.
And so the prince married her and the pea was installed
in a museum for safekeeping.

Andersen signs off this tale with an ironic 'there, that
was a true story'.

THE SWINEHERD

Being a 'real' princess in the fairy-tale world of Hans Christian Andersen means nothing if you're not a nice princess. This refreshingly different, if morally dubious, tale tells the story of a poor prince with just a small kingdom who wishes to marry the daughter of an emperor. His greatest treasures are a rose tree, upon which an exceptional single rose blooms every five years, and a nightingale whose singing is the sweetest every heard. He sends these prized possessions to his beloved as a mark of his affection.

Now, the princess is characterised as a cretin from the outset. She is disgusted that the presents the prince has sent her are 'natural' and 'real' – for this girl prefers artificial things. So, the heavy-handed metaphors in place, the princess refuses to see the wooing prince.

Not to be deterred, the prince makes his face very dirty and heads to the palace pretending to be a lowly servant. The emperor gives him a job taking care of the pigs. Once installed in his dirty room as 'Imperial Swineherd', the prince sets about making a fantastical cooking pot with bells that tinkle beautifully when it boils and which can also reveal what people all over the kingdom are eating for their dinner.

When the princess hears the music from this delightful contraption, she tries to buy it from the swineherd. He names his price as ten kisses from the princess – and is not open to haggling. So the princess reluctantly agrees, and gets her court-ladies to form a protective ring around them so that nobody will see her kissing the swineherd.

Next the swineherd constructs a rattle that can play any number of waltzes and jigs. Again the princess wants this wonderful thing, but the price for it is even higher – one hundred kisses.

And again the court-ladies form a protective circle, but from his balcony the emperor sees there's clearly something intriguing happening by the pigsty and ventures down to have a look. When he sees that his daughter is kissing the swineherd, he 'boxes her ears' with his slipper and throws both the princess and the swineherd out of the city.

Outside in the pouring rain, the princess bemoans the fact that she didn't just marry that handsome young prince who sent her the rose tree and the nightingale.

In any other story, this is the point at which we would expect the now enlightened princess to be rewarded with the prince revealing his identity and asking her to marry him. But not in this tale.

The swineherd does go behind a tree and, with a quick wipe of the mud off his face, transforms himself into the dignified and handsome prince – but he tells the princess that he has come to despise her because 'thou wast ready to kiss the swineherd for the sake of a trumpery plaything'. He goes back to his own kingdom and shuts the door of his palace in her face.

What became of the princess, we're not told.

Punishing princesses
It is unusual in fairy tales for a princess to be thus left in the lurch – even though she may suffer horribly throughout, she normally gets her 'happy ever after' at the end of a story. But, when her cruel fate is at the hands of the man who purports to love and want to marry her, the happy ending is rather hard to swallow – and the 'message' of the story pretty horrible for the women concerned.

Men can be as sadistic and cruel as they like. Women must always be supplicant and virtuous.

Especially princesses. And ultimately, that's what a 'real' princess is meant to be – supplicant and virtuous. And that's certainly what Disney has spent decades reinforcing. Though, these days, she can at least be 'sassy' so long as she is beautiful and has the heart of an angel.

In *King Thrushbeard* by the Grimms, we again see a disguised prince 'wooing' a princess. In this story, which has much in common thematically with Shakespeare's misogynistic *Taming of the Shrew*, the princess publicly humiliates all her suitors, including a young king who has a thick beard. She compares his jutting chin to a thrush's beak. (Now, let's pause to recap on her crime – she said the young king's beard looked like a thrush's beak, and then after that people started to call him 'Thrushbeard'. Time to see how proportionate the men of the tale's responses are to her crimes…)

The princess's father is enraged by her behaviour and vows that the first man to come to the palace the next day will marry her with his blessing.

The conversation is overheard by an unknown stranger and the next day a clean-shaven young minstrel comes to court and the king offers him his daughter's hand. Their marriage is delayed as the minstrel gripes that the princess doesn't look able for hard work. Needless to say, the princess herself is horrified at the match but has no choice in the matter.

The minstrel takes her away to his home, passing through the lands owned by King Thrushbeard, who the princess now regrets scorning. The minstrel's house is a hovel and he treats his prospective new wife harshly – making her work for the first time in her life. She can't do any of the tasks he sets her and so he sends her off to King Thrushbeard's castle to work as a servant. She manages to get over her humiliation and becomes a nicer person, working hard and even sharing her meagre food with hungry mice.

Then she hears that her master the king is getting married. There is a rather unfortunate event in which she is forced to dance in the great hall and her pockets burst open, showing that she has been stashing table scraps in them. She is so mortified that she bursts into tears. Thereupon, the minstrel shows up and asks why she is crying on her wedding day.

So it's revealed that the minstrel is King Thrushbeard who tells her: 'I did all that to humble your proud spirit and to punish you for the insolent way you behaved towards me.'

Properly broken or 'humbled', the princess answers, 'I've done a great wrong and do not deserve to be your wife.'

They marry, there is rejoicing and the promise of a happy-ever-after.

And if you thought that was bad...

In Giambattista Basile's *Pride Punished* (1634), the proud princess Cinziella is wooed by a king, whom she rejects with unnecessary cruelty. He then vows revenge and returns to the palace in disguise to work as a gardener. As per *The Swineherd*, this king-in-disguise dupes the princess with something pretty and unique, in this case a fabulous robe – its cost is that the gardener sleeps one night in her drawing room.

The next day, he gets into her ante-chamber with a fabulous dress and the third day a striking vest gets him into her bedroom itself. On this third night, she instructs the gardener that he is to sleep on the floor, and draws a dividing line he must not cross. But, when she is asleep, the king-slash-gardener gets into bed with her and has sex with her while she's asleep. We are told that the princess 'accepted the misdeed and found pleasure in the fault'.

She begins an affair with the gardener and becomes pregnant. The only option is for them to leave the kingdom – meaning a life in very reduced circumstances for the princess.

Returning to his own kingdom and getting his mother to be complicit in his continued trickery, the king installs his pregnant mistress in a stable and there leads her a miserable life. One day, he suggests she steal some bread, and 'catches' her, dressed as the king, calls her a 'shameless hussy' and encourages everyone to mock her. He does this again, encouraging her in one guise to steal some scraps of material and in the other calling her out as a thief.

It is only when she goes into labour that her sort-of mother-in-law insists that she be treated better and she is installed in a royal chamber where she gives birth to twin boys.

But the delightful king cannot help himself in his cruelty and the moment she has given birth starts ranting: 'Is this the bed for a low drab? Here, beat her out of this quickly, and then fumigate the room with rosemary to take away the stink.'

His mother again intercedes and says that enough is enough. And so we're told that 'happiness' ensued. Basile ends his tale with the moral that 'ruin is the daughter of pride'.

There are no words to articulate my horror.

CHAPTER 4

CRIME AND PUNISHMENT: EXECUTION, SACRIFICE, CANNIBALISM AND OTHER ACTS OF CRUELTY

'Every fairy tale had a bloody lining. Every one had teeth and claws.'   – Alice Hoffman, fantasy writer

Worrying about how the messages in our culture shape children's thoughts and behaviour isn't a new concern. It's something that the Brothers Grimm themselves addressed in their story *How Children Played at Slaughtering*. Ironically, they illustrate how children can be gruesomely influenced by the world they live in by framing it within a gruesome tale of dubious morality. So gruesome was it, in fact, that they only published it once, in their first collection in 1812, before excising it from all future editions. There really wasn't any other way of sanitising this particular horror show.

Children love to act out adult professions, like 'Doctors and Nurses', for example. In this story, we're told of a group of children between the ages of five and six who are acting out the preparation of a meal. One child is nominated to be butcher, one to be cook, one the cook's assistant and another to be a pig. We're told that the little boy playing the pig has his throat slit, while the cook's assistant catches the blood in a bowl to make sausages.

The children are caught at their gruesome game too late and the 'butcher' is brought to the mayor – who summons his council immediately. They are at a loss as to what to do until one 'wise' old man suggests a rather bizarre trial in which the butcher boy is offered a shiny red apple with one hand and a 'Rhenish gulden' (a gold coin) with the other. If the boy takes the apple, he is to be set free. If he chooses the gulden, he is to be killed. Presumably, this test is to demonstrate that the boy is an innocent who prizes an apple over gold – but what it actually proves is anyone's guess. He chooses the apple 'with a laugh' and is set free without any punishment.

Unusually, a very specific location is given for this story – so that it reads more like a news report than any-thing else.

In a second story, presented alongside the first, two boys watch their father slaughter a pig and thereafter imitate him in a game – one little boy slitting the other's throat. Their mother, who is bathing another child in the house, sees what is happening, rushes out, takes the knife from her poor dead son's throat and stabs his killer, her other son, in the heart. When she returns to tend to her child in the bath, she finds that he has drowned. Unable to cope with the trauma, she hangs herself. Her husband returns to this unspeakable scene and dies of sorrow shortly afterwards.

In this chapter, we'll look at a further selection of nursery rhymes and fairy tales on the theme of crime and punishment – a veritable smorgasbord of cruel and unusual acts – and what they tell young minds about the world around them.

PART I: NURSERY RHYMES

Ireland doesn't have many indigenous 'nursery rhymes', but there is one very special one on the subject of crime and punishment that haunted my Dublin childhood. It's called *The River Saile* and tells the strange story of an old woman, a baby and a hanging...

THE RIVER SAILE

There was an old woman and she lived in the woods,
weile weile waile.
There was an old woman and she lived in the woods,
down by the River Saile.

She had a baby three months old, weile weile waile.
She had a baby three months old, down by
the River Saile.

She had a penknife, long and sharp, weile weile waile.
She had a penknife, long and sharp, down by
the River Saile.

She stuck the penknife in the baby's heart,
weile weile waile.
She stuck the penknife in the baby's heart,
down by the River Saile.

There were three loud knocks come a'knocking on the
door, weile weile waile.
There were three loud knocks come a'knocking on the
door, down by the River Saile.

There were two policemen and a man, weile weile waile.
There were two policemen and a man,
down by the River Saile.

They took her away and they put her in the jail,
weile weile waile.
They took her away and they put her in the jail,
down by the River Saile.

They put a rope around her neck, weile weile waile.
They put a rope around her neck,
down by the River Saile.

They pulled the rope and she got hung,
weile weile waile.
They pulled the rope and she got hung,
down by the River Saile.

And that was the end of the woman in the woods,
weile weile waile.
And that was the end of the baby too,
down by the River Saile.

This rhyme was classified as a 'murder ballad' by American folklorist Francis James Child in 1896, in the category of 'the cruel mother'. Child found thirteen versions of the ballad in which children are dispatched in a variety of horrible ways, from stabbing with a penknife to being buried alive to death by strangulation. Rest assured, the murderous mothers reliably gets their comeuppance at the end every time.

COCK A DOODLE DOO

Cock a doodle doo!
My dame has lost her shoe,

My master's lost his fiddling stick,
And doesn't know what to do.

Featuring a familiar refrain from childhood, the nonsense rhyme *Cock a Doodle Doo* is connected to an Elizabethan case of child murder. Indeed, it made its first appearance in a 1606 'murder pamphlet', which described the crime in lurid detail.

The story goes that a wealthy farmer and his wife were murdered by robbers at their home and their children were kidnapped. Rather than kill the children themselves, the robbers passed them (a boy of three and a girl of four) to the dubious wife of an innkeeper to dispatch.

The boy was murdered in front of his sister, whose tongue was cut out to stop her talking about what she'd seen. The girl then appears to have escaped, been sold or otherwise misplaced. She showed up again a few years later and was adopted by a kindly local woman.

One day, while a group of children were chanting *Cock a Doodle Doo*, the little tongueless girl miraculousy joined in. She then went on to identify her brother's killers as the innkeeper's wife and her son, who were arrested and executed for their crimes.

AS I WAS GOING BY CHARING CROSS

As I was going by Charing Cross,
I saw a black man upon a black horse;
They told me it was King Charles the First –
Oh dear, my heart was ready to burst!

Moving from murder to execution, this rhyme refers to an equestrian statue of Charles I located at London's Charing Cross (near modern-day Trafalgar Square).

Charles was executed with little public support not far from Charing Cross by order of the puritans controlling the House of Commons under Oliver Cromwell (see *There Was a Crooked Man*, p103). And thus the exclamation of sorrow in the last line refers to this brutal act.

It was published as *Ride a Cock Horse* in 1804:

Ride a Cock Horse,
To Charing Cross,
To see a black man,
Upon a black horse.

The rhyme follows the same pattern as the infinitely more congenial:

Ride a cock-horse to Banbury Cross,
To see a fine lady upon a white horse;

Rings on her fingers and bells on her toes,
And she shall have music wherever she goes.

The 'fine lady' of this verse has variously been identified as Queen Elizabeth I (1533–1603), Lady Godiva (an eleventh-century noblewoman who reportedly rode naked through the streets of Coventry) and Celia Fiennes (1662–1741, a pioneering lady traveller).

ORANGES AND LEMONS

Oranges and lemons,
Say the bells of St Clement's.

You owe me five farthings,
Say the bells of St Martin's.

When will you pay me?
Say the bells of Old Bailey.

When I grow rich,
Say the bells of Shoreditch.

When will that be?
Say the bells of Stepney.

I do not know,
Says the great bell of Bow.

Here comes a candle to light you to bed,
And here comes a chopper to chop off your head.

A tune for a square dance called 'Oringes and Lemons' dates from 1665, while the first written version of the rhyme appeared in 1745. The famous old church bells rhymed off are dotted around London, and, though some were damaged in the Great Fire of 1666, they were rebuilt and all survive to the present day.

Later versions feature an additional last stanza:

Chip, chop, chip, chop,
The last man's dead.

It is widely agreed that this verse is about execution. The bells' questions are addressed to a condemned man, and church bells would toll when there was to be a public execution. These took place at Tyburn near present-day Marble Arch in London until 1783 (the gallows was nicknamed the 'Tyburn Tree'). They then moved to outside Newgate Prison. The bells of 'Old Bailey' would ring for Newgate executions. There is no church called Old Bailey, but rather it is the church of St Sepulchre, which stands on the street called Old Bailey, where the

Central Criminal Court is located on the former site of Newgate Prison. Executions took place outside Newgate until 1868 and always drew a large crowd. Afterwards, executions were brought inside the prison gate, denying many blood-thirsty Londoners a favourite pastime.

The question 'When will you pay me?' refers to the fact that Newgate was a debtors' prison. The answer 'When I grow rich / Say the bells of Shoreditch' can be read as 'never' as Shoreditch was a very poor area – and thus the condemned man had no chance of paying his debt of 'five farthings'.

The second last line ('Here comes the candle…') is thought to refer to a ritual at Newgate where the bell man of St Sepulchre would walk past the cells of the condemned carrying a candle and ringing a bell to indicate that they would be killed the following day.

This action rhyme is sung by children as they stand facing each other, their hands joined to form an arch while other children pass underneath. The child unfortunate enough to pass under the arch on the last line, falls victim to the 'chopper' – and so the children playfully mimic execution by decapitation.

All in all, quite a gruesome little ditty.

REMEMBER, REMEMBER THE 5TH OF NOVEMBER

Remember, remember the 5th of November
Gunpowder, treason and plot;
I see no reason why gunpowder treason,
Should ever be forgot.

Guy Fawkes, Guy Fawkes, it was his intent
To blow up the King and the Parliament;
Three score barrels of powder below,
Poor old England to overthrow.

By God's providence he was catch'd
With dark lantern and lighted match;
Holler boys, holler boys, make the bells ring,
Holler boys, holler boys, God save the King.

This rhyme is a wonderful piece of pro-monarchy propaganda, which spread like wildfire up and down England in the seventeenth century.

The Gunpowder Plot it relates was hatched back in 1605 by a group of disgruntled English Catholics, headed by a man called Robert Catesby. Their aim was to blow up the House of Lords at the State Opening of Parliament when the king, various other members of the royal family and a whole host of aristocrats would be present. And they came very close to succeeding. The

king in question was James I of England (also known as
James VI of Scotland) – the first Stuart monarch who
took the throne after the passing of Elizabeth I (also see
The Lion and the Unicorn on p102). Although he was the
son of the Catholic Mary, Queen of Scots, James was
a Protestant, albeit a moderate one. He was Elizabeth's
only real hope of keeping England Protestant – so she
named him as her heir.

Guy Fawkes was just one of thirteen Catholic plotters,
but he was the man in charge of lighting the fuse. He
was captured in the undercroft of Westminster Palace –
home to the House of Lords – in the early hours of 5
November ready to set off enough gunpowder to take
out the whole building.

The fifth of November is celebrated nationally as
Bonfire Night where effigies of Fawkes, known as 'Guys'
are burned atop the pyre (for the pagan origins of Bonfire
Night, see *Jack be Nimble* p26). It's a pretty brutal tradition –
and one in which young children are actively encouraged
to take part. Indeed, it is the established task of children
to make the Guy for the fire, asking passersby to donate
a 'penny for the Guy'.

Guy Fawkes was not actually burned at the stake – that
practice went out with the Tudors. Instead, he was hung,
drawn and quartered – and his head placed on a spike at
the Tower of London for the ravens to feast on.

LONDON BRIDGE IS FALLING DOWN

London Bridge is falling down,
Falling down, falling down.
London Bridge is falling down,
My fair lady.

Build it up with wood and clay,
Wood and clay, wood and clay,
Build it up with wood and clay,
My fair lady.

Wood and clay will wash away,
Wash away, wash away,
Wood and clay will wash away,
My fair lady.

Build it up with bricks and mortar,
Bricks and mortar, bricks and mortar,
Build it up with bricks and mortar,
My fair lady.

Bricks and mortar will not stay,
Will not stay, will not stay,
Bricks and mortar will not stay,
My fair lady.

Build it up with iron and steel,
Iron and steel, iron and steel,
Build it up with iron and steel,
My fair lady.

Iron and steel will bend and bow,
Bend and bow, bend and bow,
Iron and steel will bend and bow,
My fair lady.

Build it up with silver and gold,
Silver and gold, silver and gold,
Build it up with silver and gold,
My fair lady.

Silver and gold will be stolen away,
Stolen away, stolen away,
Silver and gold will be stolen away,
My fair lady.

Set a man to watch all night,
Watch all night, watch all night,
Set a man to watch all night,
My fair lady.

Suppose the man should fall asleep,
Fall asleep, fall asleep,

Suppose the man should fall asleep?
My fair lady.

Give him a pipe to smoke all night,
Smoke all night, smoke all night,
Give him a pipe to smoke all night,
My fair lady.

'London Bridge' is the name given to a river crossing at a specific part of the Thames – joining the City of London on the north bank with Southwark on the south. There have been many London Bridges. The first dates from the Roman occupation of London and would have been built from wood and clay. A later bridge was destroyed by Danish invaders in the tenth century, rebuilt by the Saxons and destroyed again in the early eleventh. It was rebuilt by the conquering Normans shortly thereafter, and destroyed again by a freak tornado in 1091. It was rebuilt again and destroyed by fire in 1136. Its next incarnation in wood was completed in 1163. It was then rebuilt in stone by order of Henry II. Opened in 1209, it featured a chapel on it dedicated to the king's former friend Thomas Becket, the Archbishop of Canterbury, whose murder he ordered. This chapel became the starting point for the pilgrimage to Becket's Canterbury shrine. Over the next hundred years or so, the bridge was crowded with houses and shops. In 1358, 138 shops were known to operate on the bridge. By the Tudor era, there were some two hundred, with some up to seven storeys tall.

Buildings on the bridge were burned during the Peasants' Revolt of 1381 and Jack Cade's rebellion of 1450, and another fire in 1633 destroyed a large portion at the north end. This last fire actually helped stop the Great Fire of 1666 spreading across the bridge to the other side of the Thames as there was nothing there to conduct the flames.

The southern gatehouse of the bridge was not a welcoming place. Since the head of William Wallace (aka Braveheart) was displayed there in 1305, it was the site where traitors' heads were impaled (often dipped in tar and boiled to preserve them). Other notable heads displayed include Jack Cade in 1450, Thomas More in 1535 and Thomas Cromwell in 1540. In 1598, Paul Hentzner, a German visitor to London whose notebooks provide a fascinating insight into London life at the time, counted thirty heads on display on the bridge. Festive!

The bridge was a hazardous place and very difficult for all but foot traffic to traverse. Between 1758 and 1762, all houses and shops on the bridge were demolished, and the bridge was widened. By the end of the eighteenth century, it was clear that the now 600-plus-year-old bridge needed to be entirely replaced.

The replacement bridge opened in 1831 and the old one was demolished shortly thereafter. This new bridge was not fit for the huge amount of traffic across it though – and was shown to be sinking slightly on the east side. It too needed to be replaced. The current rather functional and uninspiring London Bridge was opened in 1973.

It is hypothesised that, because of the difficulty in building a lasting bridge to span the Thames, a pre-Christian practice of sacrificing a child (or children) and burying them (possibly alive) in the foundations may have been part of the building of at least one of the early bridges. The theory being that the soul of the sacrificed person will protect the structure. It is suggested that the 'fair lady' or the 'watchman' of the song might be one of these sacrificed souls. This theory was first advanced by Alice Bertha Gomme (later Lady Gomme) in *The Traditional Games of England, Scotland and Ireland* (1894–98).

In an alternate version, there is a second verse, which lends weight to this theory. It goes:

> Take a key and lock her up,
> Lock her up, lock her up.

However, no skeletons have shown up during the successive rebuildings of the bridge to confirm this theory.

The rhyme is sung as part of a game similar to *Oranges and Lemons*, with its 'chopper' theme at the end (see p144). Children line up and form a series of arches, as others pass singly down the line. At the end of the song, the arches are lowered to 'catch' and decapitate a player – this may be meant to evoke the decapitated heads on spikes that once adorned the old bridge's south end.

London Bridge, Arizona
The unfit 1831 London Bridge was dismantled and sold to a wealthy American oil baron from Missouri called Robert P. McCulloch for nearly $2.5 million. McCulloch had it shipped to Lake Havasu City in Arizona where it was reconstructed and opened in 1971.

EENY, MEENY, MINY, MO

> Eeny, meeny, miny, mo,
> Catch a tiger by the toe.
> If he hollers, let him go,
> Eeny, meeny, miny, mo.

This innocent-seeming counting game, used to decide who is 'it' (who goes seeking rather than hiding, for example), has a rather terrifying history. It is thought that Celtic Druids chanted something similar – 'eena, meena, mina, mo' – to decide who would be sacrificed when human sacrifice was deemed necessary to appease the gods.

A Cornish version collected in 1882 begins: 'Ena, mena,

mona, mite', hinting at the continuation of this tradition in the old Celtic language.

The version I used as a child was pretty repellent for different reasons. Instead of tiger, we used 'nigger' who 'squeals' rather than 'hollers' when caught by the toe. This was presumably handed down from parents to children in the homogenously white 1970s Ireland I was born into.

Other variations of those caught by the toe, include tinkers, spiders and monkeys.

LITTLE BO-PEEP

Little Bo-Peep has lost her sheep,
And doesn't know where to find them;
Leave them alone, and they'll come home,
Wagging their tails behind them.

Little Bo-Peep fell fast asleep,
And dreamt she heard them bleating;
But when she awoke, she found it a joke,
For they were still a-fleeting.

Then up she took her little crook,
Determined for to find them;
She found them indeed, but it made her heart bleed,
For they'd left their tails behind them.

It happened one day, as Bo-Peep did stray
Into a meadow hard by,
There she espied their tails side by side,
All hung on a tree to dry.
She heaved a sigh and wiped her eye,
And over the hillocks went rambling,
And tried what she could, as a shepherdess should,
To tack each again to its lambkin.

Moving on to seemingly random acts of extreme cruelty, this charming little rhyme about mutilated lambs is meant to accompany children's hide-and-seek games and to teach children a lesson about falling asleep on the job. It is thought to be one of the oldest nursery rhymes around.

DING DONG BELL

Ding, dong, bell,
Pussy's in the well.
Who put her in?
Little Johnny Flynn.
Who pulled her out?
Little Tommy Stout.
What a naughty boy was that,
To try to drown poor pussy cat,
Who ne'er did him any harm,
But killed all the mice in the farmer's barn.

Thankfully, no cats were harmed in the making of this nursery rhyme. Sadly, the same can't be said of the rhyme upon which it is based, first recorded in 1580 by John Lant, organist of Winchester Cathedral:

> Jacke boy, ho boy newes,
> The cat is in the well,
> Let us ring now for her Knell,
> Ding dong ding dong Bell.

SING A SONG OF SIXPENCE

But animals occasionally get their revenge. In *Sing a Song of Sixpence*, which is tenuously linked to Henry VIII and the dissolution of the monasteries again, an unfortunate woman is savaged by a blackbird at the end, presumably exacting revenge for his brothers who are eaten in a pie…

> Sing a song of sixpence,
> A pocket full of rye.
> Four and twenty blackbirds,
> Baked in a pie.
>
> When the pie was opened,
> The birds began to sing;
> Wasn't that a dainty dish,
> To set before the king?

The king was in his counting house,
Counting out his money;
The queen was in the parlour,
Eating bread and honey.

The maid was in the garden,
Hanging out the clothes,
When down came a blackbird
And pecked off her nose.

The final line of the fourth verse sometimes varies, with the unfortunate maiden's nose either being 'pecked' or 'nipped' off. One of the following additional verses is sometimes added to take the edge off the savage and abrupt ending, denying justice to the blackbirds:

They sent for the king's doctor,
Who sewed it on again;
He sewed it on so neatly,
The seam was never seen.

Or

There was such a commotion,
That little Jenny Wren
Flew down into the garden,
And put it back again.

PART II: FAIRY TALES

Moving away from the gratuitous gruesomeness of nursery rhymes, in this section, we'll look at some of the fairy-tale world's most beloved criminals, including Jack (of the Beanstalk fame) and the porridge thief and despoiler of furniture, Goldilocks – and the kind of role models they represent for young readers.

JACK AND THE BEANSTALK

This English fairy tale first appeared in print in 1807 in *Popular Stories for the Nursery* by Benjamin Tabart (1767–1833).

It was subsequently popularised by Felix Summerly (pen name of Henry Cole, 1808–82) in *The Home Treasury* (1842). But the best-known version is by influential folklorist Joseph Jacobs (1854–1916), in his *English Fairy Tales* (1890).

From 1890 to 1916, Jacobs edited and contributed to numerous collections of fairy tales. As well as *English Fairy Tales*, Jacobs collected *Celtic Fairy Tales* (1892), *Indian Fairy Tales* (1912) and *European Folk and Fairy Tales* (1916). In addition to his fairy tales, Jacobs published many scholarly works on the subject of Judaism and Jewish history.

English Fairy Tales features other uniquely English tales

such as *The Story of the Three Bears* (p171), *Jack the Giant Killer* (p164), *The History of Tom Thumb* and *Whittington and His Cat*.

Jacobs' *Jack and the Beanstalk* is considered to be closer to the older oral versions of the tale than Tabart's tale – as the latter included quite a lot of additional moralising in his text. Jacobs said of this story, 'I tell this as it was told me in Australia, somewhere about the year 1860.'

In Jacobs' tale, a poor widow lives with her son Jack and their cow Milky White. The cow is the family's only source of income and, one morning, when she doesn't provide any milk, they resolve to sell her on the market. On his way to sell the cow, Jack bumps into a strange-looking old man on the road, to whom he sells the cow for five 'magic' beans. The old man tells him that when planted they will grow overnight into a tall plant that reaches the sky. Jack needs little persuasion and hands Milky over.

When his mother hears of this transaction she whips him soundly and sends him to bed without supper, before throwing the beans out the window in disgust.

When Jack wakes the following morning, he sees that a gigantic beanstalk that reaches to the sky has grown just as the old man said it would. Jack excitedly leaps from his bedroom window on to the beanstalk and begins to climb.

When he gets to the top, he finds a road leading to a

big, tall house, with a hugely tall woman standing upon its doorstep. Jack walks straight up to her and asks if she might give him some breakfast.

She tells him, 'It's breakfast you'll be if you don't move off from here. My man is an ogre and there's nothing he likes better than boys broiled on toast. You'd better be moving on or he'll be coming.'

But Jack begs her for some food, claiming he'll die of hunger. The ogress softens, and brings him in for some bread, cheese and milk. But no sooner has Jack finished his meal than the house begins to tremble with the noise of the giant ogre approaching. The panicked ogress gets Jack to hide in the oven for safety.

The ogre is a huge creature and has three calves hanging from his belt, which he presents to his wife to cook for his breakfast. But then, he smells something in the air...

Fee-fi-fo-fum!
I smell the blood of an Englishman,
Be he alive, or be he dead,
I'll grind his bones to make my bread.

His wife dismisses his olfactory musings, suggesting that it may just be the scraps of the little boy he ate for his dinner the day before that he now smells. She sends the ogre off to wash while she prepares breakfast.

161

After he's eaten, the ogre takes a couple of bags of gold from a chest and counts out his money before falling asleep and snoring loudly. Jack creeps out of the oven, grabs one of the bags of gold and steals off down the beanstalk.

Jack and his mother live off this swag for a while. But when it runs out Jack resolves to climb the beanstalk once more.

Again, the ogre is away and Jack sweet-talks his wife, denying any knowledge of the missing bag of gold. Once again, the ogre returns as Jack is eating and the boy hides in the oven. This time, the ogre toys with a hen (a goose in other tellings) that lays golden eggs before again nodding off to sleep, giving Jack the opportunity to steal from him once more.

But as Jack is sneaking off with the hen it squawks, waking the ogre but not in time to catch him. Jack races down the beanstalk and presents the hen to his mother, demonstrating how it lays golden eggs on command.

Jack next decides to climb the beanstalk, not because the hen has stopped laying, but because he's clearly got a taste for thievery. This time, he does not go straight to the house but waits till the ogress leaves to fetch water before he sneaks in. But soon both the ogress and her husband return. The ogre smells the 'blood of an Englishman' again and this time his wife is onside. The two rush to the oven, but Jack is not hiding there. The wife concludes that the smell must be from the boy her husband caught the night before.

But still the ogre does a sweep search just in case – looking everywhere but Jack's hiding place. The ogre eats his breakfast and calls on his wife to bring him his gold harp – an instrument that sings beautifully on demand.

When the ogre predictably falls asleep, Jack creeps from his hiding place, grabs the harp and dashes to the door. But the harp calls out 'Master! Master!' waking the ogre just in time to see Jack running out. He gives chase and follows Jack down the beanstalk. When he is near the ground Jack calls to his mother to bring him an axe – he lands and immediately starts chopping. The beanstalk is halved and, echoing *Jack and Jill* (p184), we're told 'then the ogre fell down and broke his crown, and the beanstalk came toppling after'.

Between demonstrations of the singing harp and selling the golden eggs, Jack and his mother become rich. Jack marries a princess and the two live happily ever after.

Origins

A comic variant of the tale is found in the 1734 edition of *Round About Our Coal-Fire* – a book of 'entertainments' – under the title *The Story of Jack Spriggins and the Enchanted Bean*.

The ogre's cry 'Fee! Fie! Foe! Fum!' is also found in Shakespeare's *King Lear* (written c. 1603) as 'Fie, foh, and fum, I smell the blood of a British man', showing that the refrain, and very likely the story, had been around for a while.

Attempts have been made to connect *Jack and the Beanstalk* to other European tales, usually those featuring giants, but there aren't any close relatives in evidence, other than another English tale *Jack the Giant Killer*.

Giants and those who do battle with them have a long folk history in Cornish, Breton, Welsh and Gaelic lore. Folklorists Iona and Peter Opie also suggest that the 'Jack and Giant' tales share similarities with Norse myths.

Jack the Giant Killer didn't appear in print until 1711. But the fact that folklore abounds with tales of giant-slaying and that this story is set during King Arthur's reign hint at a considerably earlier origin.

Jack is the son of a Cornish farmer who encounters Cormoran (The Giant of the Sea). Cormoran devours cattle and generally menaces people. Jack lures Cormoran into a trap – a deep pit – and there dispatches him with a pickaxe. When Cormoran's brother giants get wind of this, they come after Jack, only to be slain as well. Jack also kills a two-headed Welsh giant along the way.

Jack then becomes the servant of King Arthur's son, with whom he encounters a three-headed giant. And, after saving the prince, is gifted with a magic sword, cap of knowledge, invisibility cloak and swift shoes – all of which come in handy on his subsequent giant-slaying adventures. Jack ultimately becomes a member of the Round Table of King Arthur and marries the daughter of a duke.

Again the refrain 'Fee, fau, fum' features in the 1711 tale.

The moral of the story?
At its most fundamental, *Jack and the Beanstalk* is a tale about a young man who breaks into another man's home, gains the sympathy of the man's wife, hides there, repeatedly robs the man and then kills him. What makes Jack a 'hero' is simply the fact that he is a human and not a cannibalistic giant.

Keenly aware of this dodgy morality, Benjamin Tabart inserted a fairy woman into the first printed version of the story to tell Jack that the giant had previously robbed then killed his father – therefore giving him the green light for revenge.

In 2001, the Jim Henson Company produced a miniseries called *Jack and the Beanstalk: The Real Story*. This retelling focuses on Jack's dubious morality and motivations, characterising the giant as a friendly creature. When a descendant, Jack Robinson (played by Matthew Modine), learns what his forebear was guilty of, he resolves to return the golden egg-laying goose and magical harp to the giants' kingdom.

The 2013 film *Jack the Giant Slayer* blends the tales

of the beanstalk and the giant killer together with a liberal dash of Hollywood pixie dust. In this tale, an unassuming farmhand is propelled into an outlandish adventure where he must rescue a princess from the land of the giants. In this film, the giants are a pretty nasty bunch determined to wipe out mankind and Jack is also given a human bad guy to deal with (played with scenery-chewing glee by Stanley Tucci) – thus allowing his virtues to shine even brighter.

The Giant's Causeway

A geometric and geological wonder, the Giant's Causeway in Co Antrim, Northern Ireland, was formed millions of years ago from lava following a volcanic eruption. Its strange basalt columns are associated with an equally strange legend involving one of the best-known figures of Irish mythology, Fionn mac Cumhaill. Legend has it that mac Cumhaill, who was giant in stature, built the Causeway so that he could cross the sea to Scotland to do battle with another fierce giant Benandonner.

When mac Cumhaill realised that Benandonner was even more giant than him, his wife disguised him as a baby and he got into a cradle in their home. When Benandonner came looking for the missing mac Cumhaill and saw the size of his supposed offspring, he fled in fear, assuming that mac Cumhaill, as the father of such a gargantuan child, must be very giant indeed.

Benandonner then destroyed the Causeway to ensure that mac Cumhaill couldn't follow him.

Across the sea, on the Scottish isle of Staffa lies Fingal's Cave, where identical basalt columns were formed by the same lava as the Giant's Causeway – 'proving' the existence of this one-time bridge.

HOP O' MY THUMB

Though this story more often invites comparisons with *Hansel and Gretel*, it shares a great many similarities with the Jack stories: a poor boy is pitied and fed by an ogre's wife; the ogre smells him out with the intention of eating him; and the boy then steals from the ogre while he is sleeping.

Written in 1697 by Charles Perrault, the tale is similar to *Hansel and Gretel* in that a woodcutter and his wife elect to abandon their seven sons in the woods when they're low on cash and facing starvation. One of these young boys, called 'Hop o' My Thumb' because of his small size and quiet nature, has long been thought of as stupid by his parents, but in fact is the canniest of their offspring. When Hop hears the two of them discussing their situation and the decision to abandon their children, he comes up with a plan to find his way home again.

Hop fills his pockets with white pebbles from the garden, which he uses to leave a trail to follow back home from the dark part of the woods where he and his brothers are left. When Hop and Co return to the house, he listens at the door first to hear his regretful parents bewailing their rash decision as some money they are owed has just come in. They are therefore overjoyed to see their boys are alive and returned.

Things are all right for a time, but, when the money runs out again, the watchful Hop learns that his parents once again plan to abandon them in the woods – and to do a better job of losing them this time. The night before the abandonment is to occur, the parents lock the door, preventing Hop from gathering his white pebbles.

However, when the parents give their sons a piece of bread each for the journey, Hop leaves a trail of breadcrumbs – but, alas, the birds eat them all up so the boys are indeed well and truly lost.

As the boys wander the dark woods in terror, Hop sees a distant light and guides his brothers to the house that holds it.

There, a kindly woman takes them in to give them food. However, she warns them that her husband is an ogre who eats little children. Hop and his brothers decide to take their chances at the ogre's house rather than outside with the forest wolves.

When the ogre's wife hears her husband returning, she hides the boys under the bed but it's not long before her carnivorous other half smells 'fresh meat' and catches them. The ogre's wife manages to convince her husband not to kill them immediately, but to do it in the morning. The boys are put to bed in the same room as the ogre's seven little daughters – all of whom are fast asleep and, like their father, eat human meat. Perrault describes them as having small eyes, hooked noses and big mouths with long sharp teeth for biting children and sucking their blood.

Now, each one of these little ogresses is wearing a golden crown and Hop has the idea of swapping these crowns for his and his brothers' caps by way of a disguise, for he suspects that the ogre may not be able to wait till morning to start his butchering.

He's right of course, and a little later in comes the ogre, feeling around in the dark for his victims. He leaves the seven little heads with the crowns on alone, but when he feels the caps he starts slicing. He cuts all seven throats and returns to bed. Hop then rouses his brothers and they run off into the relative safety of the woods.

The ogre is naturally upset when he wakes up to find his daughters accidentally slain. He dons his 'seven league boots' (an item of footwear that pops up in fairy tales from time to time and allows the wearer to cover great distances in a short time). He sets out to find Hop and Co and picks up their track near to their parents' house. The boys manage to hide from the ogre in the hollow of a rock. When the exhausted killer takes a nap, Hop sends his brothers scurrying back to their 'loving' parents, while he sets about stealing the ogre's boots.

He eases them off the ogre and slips them on (they magically shrink to fit) and then he races back to the ogre's house, where he tells the wife that her husband is being held by robbers who are demanding all his silver and gold as ransom. She hands over the loot and Hop returns home with enough money to stop his parents trying to off them in the woods again.

Perrault 'interjects' at the end of the story to say that 'there are many people who disagree about this last incident', i.e. Hop stealing the ogre's silver and gold. But he confirms that he definitely stole the magic boots and used them to become a courier to the king, amassing great wealth in this profession.

I guess the moral here is that it's OK to arrange for the killing of seven ogre children and to steal from their murderous ogre father, but it's not OK to steal from his kindly wife.

In his own moral at the end of the story, Perrault interprets it as demonstrating that being small isn't always a disadvantage.

Hop's parents escape judgement for their own cruel behaviour, abandoning their children not once, but twice – until the children have to effectively bribe them into keeping them!

THE STORY OF THE THREE BEARS

The first recorded version of this tale was a relatively recent find, showing up in 1951 in a collection of children's books at the Toronto Public Library. This version was a homemade effort, written and illustrated by Eleanor Mure for her nephew in 1831. In this tale, taken from an existing oral story, an old woman trespasses into the house of three benevolent male bears, eating their food and trying out/despoiling their furniture.

It was recorded again by the writer and poet Robert Southey in 1837, reaching a considerably wider audience. Again in this telling of the story, the three bears are grown-up male bears of differing sizes – little, medium and large – into whose home an old woman trespasses. The tale, entitled *The Story of the Three Bears*, was included in a collection of essays and miscellanea called *The Doctor*.

The little girl with golden hair blundering into the house of Mother, Father and Baby Bear came some years later.

At its most basic, this is a tale about stealing – and certainly in Southey's telling he's at pains to point out the wicked nature of the old woman thief and how she may have got her comeuppance. When the thief character became an adorable little girl, this moral was somewhat lost. Instead, later versions can often lack any evidence of the thief being punished or even penitent.

Southey's tale

Once upon a time, there were three bears who lived together in a house in the woods. 'One of them was a Little, Small, Wee Bear; and one was a Middle-sized Bear, and the other was a Great, Huge Bear.' They are harmless, gentle-natured bears who think well of their fellow creatures.

They each have a pot for their porridge, a chair and a bed – sized small, medium and large accordingly. One morning, the three go for a walk while their porridge cools. While they are away, an old woman wandering in the woods comes upon their house. Southey tells us, 'She could not have been a good, honest old Woman; for first she looked in at the window, and then she peeped in at the keyhole; and seeing nobody in the house, she lifted the latch.'

Seeing the porridge laid out, she helps herself. After trying the biggest bowl first and finding it too hot, she tastes the medium-sized bowl, which is too cool, before she settles on the smallest bowl, which is just right for her. We're told she says 'bad words' about each of the bowls in turn, decrying the small one for not containing enough food for her.

Once she's eaten, this nasty old woman tries out the bears' chairs. The biggest is too hard for her, the medium too soft and the little one is just right, but she manages to break it. This done, she makes her way upstairs to the bedroom and tries out the beds. The biggest and medium beds are too high for her liking so she settles in the smallest to sleep. The bears return and find that their porridge has been variously tampered with and eaten.

Next, they see that someone has been sitting in their chairs and has broken the smallest one. They venture upstairs to find the two bigger beds have been tampered with too. Peeping from the covers of the smallest bed on the pillow is the 'little old Woman's ugly, dirty head'.

Awakened in fright by the shrill voice of the smallest bear, the old woman sees the three standing over her at the side of the bed, leaps up and rushes out of the window.

The ending is inconclusive but certainly has a punitive air: 'Out the little old Woman jumped; and whether she broke her neck in the fall; or ran into the wood and was lost there; or found her way out of the wood, and was taken up by the constable and sent to the House of Correction for a vagrant as she was, I cannot tell. But the Three Bears never saw anything more of her.'

Other origins
It is thought that the tale may have originally featured a fox, rather than an old woman as in the story *Scrapefoot*, which was first recorded by Joseph Jacobs (of *Jack and the Beanstalk* fame) in 1894 and is thought to be of older origin than either Southey's and Mure's story.

In *Scrapefoot*, the bears live in a castle in the same wood as a fox called Scrapefoot. He is afraid of the bears, but very curious about them all the same, and one day decides to sneak into the castle for a look around. Again, the fox tries out the bears' three chairs, breaking the smallest; three saucers of milk, drinking all from the smallest; and three beds, falling asleep in the smallest one. But this time the bears' response to the intruder is a little more aggressive. The big bear thinks they should hang Scrapefoot, the middle bear is for drowning, and the smallest for throwing him out the window. This option wins out and the fox is thrown from the window but, luckily for him, no bones are broken upon landing. He runs home, resolving to never again return to the castle.

The breaking, entering and helping oneself theme has much in common with the tale of Snow White (see p187) – who does much the same in the house of the seven dwarves. Folklorists Iona and Peter Opie have also identified a similar Norwegian tale about a princess who seeks refuge in the cave home of three Russian princes who dress in bearskins. This hungry princess eats their food and then hides under a bed when they return.

When the victims of each girl's theft return home to find things displaced, broken and eaten, the refrain in the *Three Bears* is very similar to that in *Snow White* – alternating between the announcement that 'Someone's been sleeping in my bed' and the question 'Who's been sleeping in my bed?'

Enter Goldilocks

In their book *The Classic Fairy Tales*, Iona and Peter Opie illustrate the trajectory of the trespassing thief character from wicked old woman to golden-haired innocent. Twelve years after Robert Southey's *The Story of the Three Bears* was published, Joseph Cundall transformed the old woman character into a young girl named 'Silver Hair'. His story was published in his *Treasury of Pleasure Books for Young Children* (1849) and led to a succession of other such stories featuring 'Silver Hair' and the three bears. In 1858, the character became 'Silver-Locks' in *Aunt Mavor's Nursery Tales*. She changed to 'Golden Hair' in *Aunt Friendly's Nursery Book* (1868). But it wasn't until the twentieth century that Goldilocks was born, making her first appearance in *Old Nursery Stories and Rhymes*, illustrated by John Hassall (c. 1904).

During the same period of transformation, the bears changed from an all-male trio to being Mother, Father and Baby Bear.

Unlike that first old lady, there's no hint in the later Goldilocks tales that the girl is ever caught and punished for her transgressions. She either escapes via a window, comes close to being eaten by the angry bears but gets away/is rescued, and occasionally she vows to be a good child – learning a lesson about the dangers of wandering into a stranger's house, breaking or soiling their furniture and helping yourself to their food.

HERE COMES A CHOPPER TO CHOP OFF YOUR HEAD

In his unique retelling of famous fairy tales, *Revolting Rhymes*, Roald Dahl sums up the skewed morals of the Goldilocks story thus:

> This famous wicked little tale
> Should never have been put on sale.
> It is a mystery to me
> Why loving parents cannot see
> That this is actually a book
> About a brazen little crook.
> Had I the chance I wouldn't fail
> To clap young Goldilocks in jail.

CHAPTER 5

MODEL FAMILIES: DOMESTIC DISHARMONY, EVIL STEPMOTHERS AND CHILD ABANDONMENT

'The more one knows fairy tales the less fantastical they appear; they can be vehicles of the grimmest realism, expressing hope against all the odds with gritted teeth.'
– Marina Warner, *From the Beast to the Blonde: On Fairy Tales and Their Tellers*

It's somewhat strange that tales and rhymes told by parents to their children at bedtime so often portray the family unit as dysfunctional and sometimes downright dangerous.

In this chapter, we'll look at some pretty graphic examples of domestic violence and the mistreatment of children. We've already met Peter the pumpkin eater who imprisoned his wife and/or beat and killed her in variations on the theme; children who can only play at night because their daytime lives are spent at hard graft; and heard about babies stabbed to death by deranged old women. Now, we'll turn to the archetypes of dysfunctional families – Punch and Judy, and the old woman living in the shoe for whom a sound whipping is an answer to her problems.

Fairy tales take domestic and familial cruelty to a whole new level – repeatedly presenting situations in which the young and innocent are either cruelly mistreated or placed in situations of extreme jeopardy. So far, we've seen youngsters cursed (*Sleeping Beauty*, *The Frog King*, *Hans My Hedgehog*), menaced by metaphoric wild animals representing pederasts (*Little Red Riding Hood*), pursued for incestuous relationships (*Donkey Skin*), treated terribly as domestic drudges (*The Fairies*), and cruelly abandoned by their parents (*Hop o' My Thumb*). In this chapter, we'll examine the bleakest examples of these tales, where the cruelty of stepfamilies, especially stepmothers, is a central theme (*Cinderella*, *Snow White*), where child abandonment turns little kiddies into killers (*Hansel and Gretel*) and where innocent young brides are slaughtered on a whim (*Bluebeard*).

PART I: NURSERY RHYMES

PUNCH AND JUDY

Punch and Judy fought for a pie,
Punch gave Judy a blow in the eye;
Says Punch to Judy, 'Will you have more?'
Says Judy to Punch, 'No, my eye is too sore.'

Domestic violence is par for the course for this grotesque husband and wife duo, easily recognisable by their oversized facial features, swawking, kazoo-like voices and clownish clothes.

Their stories are simple and tend to involve Punch being asked to look after the couple's long-suffering baby, neglecting it terribly, being reprimanded by the returning Judy, and engaging in a physical fight with her involving a resounding beating with his 'slapstick'.

Often a constable might show up to stop the violence and get a good clattering himself. And occasionally a crocodile, doctor or other enemy, including the devil, might feel the wrath of Punch's bat to the delight of the cheering crowd. And we mustn't forget the ubiquitous string of sausages that tended to feature prominently in every story.

At the end, Punch and Judy usually kiss and make up. The lesson for our little ones? Fathers are inept and neglectful. And violence in a marriage is commonplace and harmless – as long as the wife gets a few punches in. That's the way you do it!

The Punch and Judy show originated in sixteenth-century Naples, Italy. Punch started life as Pulcinella, a trickster character with roots going way back to antiquity. The famous diarist Samuel Pepys was the first to report on seeing a Punch show in Covent Garden back in the 1660s. He described the marionette show as 'very pretty'. So presumably the hooked nose, protruding chin and hunchback associated with Mr Punch were not in evidence at that stage. By the eighteenth century, however, Punch and Judy were set in their types and big business in London and Bath. The shows also became popular in Paris and British-colonised America.

Continuing on the subject of domestic violence, James Orchard Halliwell's *The Nursery Rhymes of England* (1842) features a lovely days-of-the-week rhyme about wife-beating/murder:

Tom married a wife on Sunday,
Beat her well on Monday,
Bad was she on Tuesday,
Middling was she on Wednesday,
Worse was she on Thursday,
Dead was she on Friday;
Glad was Tom on Saturday night,
To bury his wife on Sunday.

A similar rhyme sees the man at the centre of the action hanged for horse theft…

> Saturday-night my wife did die,
> I buried her on Sunday,
> I courted another coming from church,
> And married her on the Monday.
> On Tuesday night I stole a horse,
> On Wednesday was apprehended,
> On Thursday I was tried and case,
> And on Friday I was hanged.

Punched and brooding

Several bands have released songs called 'Punch and Judy' about marital strife and domestic violence.

Marillion's 1984 song is a hymn to domestic dreariness, portraying a marriage gone stale and characterised by 'Single beds, middle age dread'. It also has the distinction of coining the wonderful word 'suburbanshee'.

The Stranglers explore the erotic side of the puppets' tempestuous relationship, while the Lightning Seeds' 1994 song is a grim tale of battery – 'Baby's eyes are black' – and marital breakdown – 'She's never coming back'.

THERE WAS AN OLD WOMAN WHO
LIVED IN A SHOE

There was an old woman who lived in a shoe.
She had so many children, she didn't know what to do;
She gave them some broth without any bread;
Then whipped them all soundly and put them to bed.

From child neglect and casual domestic violence to a family close to starvation for whom 'whipping' is the answer, nursery rhymes don't come much grimmer than *There Was an Old Woman Who Lived in a Shoe*. This rhyme first appeared in Joseph Ritson's *Gammer Gurton's Garland* (1794) and featured the more graphic last line: 'She whipped all their bums and sent them to bed.'

Nursery rhyme enthusiasts have linked the verse to Queen Caroline, wife of George II, a mother of eight little darlings. King George was playfully known as 'the old woman' because of his penchant for wearing white powdered wigs – and because his wife was seen as the real power behind the throne. But apart from this and the large family element there seems little else to connect the unfortunate resident of the shoe and the royal family – for whom food would certainly not have been an issue.

They're also highly unlikely to ever have had to discipline or put their own children to bed – that's what servants are for.

HUSH-A-BYE BABY

Hush-a-bye baby
On the treetop,
When the wind blows
The cradle will rock.
When the bough breaks,
The cradle will fall,
And down will fall baby
Cradle and all.

Also known as *Rock-a-Bye Baby*, this rhyme is thought to have appeared in the first edition of *Mother Goose's Melody* (c. 1765). Subsequent editions of the book feature the following somewhat daunting caveat: 'This may serve as a warning to the proud and ambitious, who climb so high that they generally fall at last.'

This 'warning' echoes the expression that 'pride comes before a fall', which has its origin in the 1611 King James translation of the Book of Proverbs in the Bible: 'Pride goeth before destruction, and a haughty spirit before a fall' (Proverbs, 16:18).

One wonders then who this haughty baby might be? There is a suggestion, though not a popular one, that the son of King James II, James Francis Edward, was a 'changeling', smuggled into the room where the Queen, Mary of Modena, was giving birth and swapped with the 'real' baby to ensure a Catholic heir to the throne. The 'wind' that blows has been interpreted as the Protestant William of Orange and the 'cradle' the House of Stuart.

Another claim is that the lullaby originated with the first white settlers of America – the Mayflower pilgrims – who emulated the Native American habit of hanging their babies in cribs from trees to be rocked to sleep by the wind.

Whatever the origin, the message of the lullaby isn't the most restful – suggesting a baby tumbling from a height, rather than drifting off to a sound sleep.

JACK AND JILL

Jack and Jill went up the hill
To fetch a pail of water.
Jack fell down and broke his crown,
And Jill came tumbling after.

Up Jack got and home did trot,
As fast as he could caper;
And went to bed and bound his head
With vinegar and brown paper.

References to characters called Jack and Jill in popular culture go back to Shakespeare in the latter half of the sixteenth century who writes that 'Jack shall have Jill;

Nought shall go ill' in *A Midsummer Night's Dream* and 'Our wooing doth not end like an old play; Jack hath not Jill' in *Love's Labour's Lost*.

The verse itself is widely considered to be a 'nonsense rhyme' – indicated from the first lines about the two performing the unlikely act of going up a hill to fetch water. However, there is one theory that the rhyme is inspired by events in France during the Reign of Terror in the 1790s. In this interpretation, Jack represents King Louis XVI, who was beheaded by guillotine in 1793 ('fell down and broke his crown'), and that Jill represents his wife Marie Antoinette, who was beheaded later in October that year ('came tumbling after'). But given the rhyme is believed to have been included in the first edition of *Mother Goose's Melody* (c. 1765) that makes this explanation rather implausible. Gruesome, but implausible.

A version dating from a nineteenth-century chapbook includes a violent third verse, turning the nonsense rhyme into yet another warning for children looking to avoid the lash:

> Then Jill came in, and she did grin,
> To see Jack's paper plaster;
> Her mother whipt her, across her knee,
> For laughing at Jack's disaster.

Another little girl who got whipped for a minor infraction was Little Polly Flinders…

LITTLE POLLY FLINDERS

Little Polly Flinders
Sat among the cinders,
Warming her pretty little toes.
Mother came and caught her,
And whipped her little daughter
For spoiling her nice new clothes.

PART II: FAIRY TALES

'Better a serpent than a stepmother'
– Euripides (c.480–406 BCE)

The biological family is presented as by far the superior social unit in fairy tales – and in-laws and stepfamilies as a source of distrust. Saying that, there are plenty of examples of biological parents mistreating their children. Remember how Rapunzel's biological mother's reckless cravings led to her being handed over to a witch as a babe in arms; how the father of the princess in *Donkey Skin* decided that their relationship should take an incestuous turn; how Beauty's father sent her to live with a beast; and how Hop o' My Thumb's parents abandoned him and his brothers in the deepest part of the dark forest when the going got tough?

But, when it comes to evil doings, stepfamilies, and stepmothers in particular, are singled out for special treatment. And, in these instances, biological fathers are usually either shown as weak-willed and ineffectual or they simply disappear from the stories altogether once the scene has been set. Mothers-in-law can be pretty horrible too – let's not forget Perrault's *Sleeping Beauty* in which the ogress queen attempts to eat both her grandchildren and her daughter-in-law. Unless they are a benevolent fairy godmother, it's difficult to find many examples in fairy tales of older women who are not characterised as ruthless, jealous and/or blood-thirsty.

SNOW WHITE

'I used to be Snow White, but I drifted.' – Mae West

In the Grimm Brothers' stories, instances of cruelty in biological mothers are a major inconvenience – and tend to be excised. In their first version of *Snow White* in 1812, for example, it was Snow White's mother, the very woman who wished for a daughter with black, white and red colouring, who then turned on her own child when she grew too pretty. And it was this same mother who commissioned her huntsman to stab the child to death in the woods and return with her liver and lungs so that she might eat them.

By their 1819 revision, the mother was recast as a gentle soul who died shortly after giving birth and was replaced within a year by the psychotically jealous stepmother character we now associate with the story.

Something similar happened between their 1812 and 1857 versions of *Hansel and Gretel* (p204), with their mother, mysteriously acquiring the prefix 'step' in the intervening years. She, after all, is the one who suggests to their father that they abandon their two children in the deep dark woods when the going gets tough…

The stepmother version

So, once upon a time, a queen is sitting sewing by a window in her palace, watching the snow falling outside. The frame of the window is as black as ebony, and, after accidentally pricking her finger, she watches as three drops of blood hit the perfect white snow outside. In her reverie, the queen wishes that she might have a daughter as white as snow, as red as blood, and as black as the wood of the window frame. And shortly after she gives birth to a little girl with just this colouring, whom she names Snow White.

And then she dies. And a year later her husband, the king, takes another wife. She is beautiful, but like all fairy-tale stepmothers is 'proud and haughty', though this particular stepmother's pride is rather extreme. She can't tolerate the idea of anyone being more beautiful than her and so regularly consults a magic mirror with the request:

> 'Mirror, mirror, on the wall,
> Who in this realm is the fairest of all?'

And the mirror duly answers:

> 'You, my queen, are the fairest of them all.'

A few years pass and by the age of seven Snow White is 'as beautiful as the day is clear and more beautiful than the queen herself'.

One day, when the queen consults her magic mirror for her usual dose of reassurance, it comes back to her with:

> You, my queen, may have a beauty quite rare,
> But Snow White is a thousand times more fair.'

The queen does not take this news well. From that moment on, she hates her stepdaughter and when the hate consumes her entirely she orders a huntsman to take Snow White into the forest, kill her and bring back her lungs and liver as proof that she is dead.

The huntsman brings the girl into the woods as bidden,

but when it comes to doing the dreadful deed he cannot – and gives in to the little girl's plea and promise that she will run into the wild forest and never come back again if he would only spare her.

He then kills a wild boar, and takes its lungs and liver out as the required proof of Snow White's passing for the queen.

When she receives the organs, gruesomely she asks her cook to boil them up for her – and then she eats them both, believing them to be Snow White's.

Meanwhile, the poor little girl is alone and lost in the forest, banished forever from her home. She wanders terrified for hours, until she finally comes across a little house.

Nobody is home, but she goes in anyway and finds everything there to be 'indescribably dainty and neat'. There is a table laid for dinner with seven little place settings. As she is so hungry, she helps herself to a little food from each plate and a little drink from each of the seven cups.

After that, she tries out each of the house's seven pristine little beds in turn, finding them alternately too long or too short, until she finally settles on one that fits just right.

When it's dark, the cottage's inhabitants return. They are seven dwarves who work as mineral miners in the mountains. They immediately notice that things are amiss and wonder aloud who has been eating their food, sitting in their chairs, using their cutlery and drinking from their cups. And finally, they notice that their beds are wrinkled from being tried out, and that someone is currently asleep in the furthest one…

Thankfully, their response to finding her is friendly. They suggest that, if she keeps house for them, she can stay.

And so they commence a new domestic routine, but, as Snow White is to be alone during the day, the dwarves warn her to be on the alert – her stepmother is sure to discover that she is still alive and living there – and so she must not let anybody in.

And indeed they are right, for when the vain queen once again consults her mirror – she learns that her stepdaughter is alive and living with the dwarves beyond the mountains.

Horrified, she immediately starts plotting Snow White's demise – something she intends to undertake personally. So she dresses as an old peddler and makes her way to the dwarves' cottage on the pretext of selling 'pretty wares'.

She has no trouble duping Snow White and she sells her a staylace for fastening her dress. The old woman then offers to tie the lace for Snow White and fastens it so tight that the girl loses her breath and collapses. Thinking her dead, the stepmother departs. The dwarves return and manage to revive Snow White by cutting the lace.

Again, they warn her to be careful of strangers, and again the queen learns that her murder attempt has been unsuccessful thanks to her trusty mirror.

Next she makes a poison comb and again disguises herself as an old woman selling pretty wares to call at the cottage. This time, Snow White is slightly more cautious, but still ultimately duped into letting the old woman in and combing her hair. She falls down as if dead the moment the comb touches her head.

But again her magic isn't powerful enough and the dwarves need only remove the comb from her hair to revive Snow White.

On her third attempt to kill her stepdaughter, the queen dresses as a peasant woman and visits the cottage pretending to be an apple seller. This time, she has cunningly poisoned a delicious-looking apple, but only one side so she can demonstrate to the girl, by tasting it herself, that the apple is fit for eating. And so she dupes the gullible Snow White into taking a bite of the poisoned half of the apple and the girl falls down dead – and this time the dwarves cannot rouse her.

When the queen next asks her mirror who is the fairest of them all – she gets the answer she wants and is restored to the number-one spot.

The dwarves are devastated and decide that Snow

White is too beautiful to be buried in the ground. Besides which, she looks like she's still alive. So they create a glass coffin for her with her name and the detail that she is a princess written in gold letters upon it. They then place the coffin at the top of a mountain and always ensure that one of them is present to guard it.

Many years pass with Snow White lying in her glass coffin with no sign of decay. Instead, she looks as though she is simply sleeping.

One day, a prince chances across the dwarves' house – from there he heads up the mountain to see the fabled glass coffin. Upon seeing it, he tells the dwarves he'll pay them whatever they want for it. They refuse but then the prince asks them to give it to him as a gift and that he can't go on living without being able to see Snow White. He promises that he will honour and cherish her as his 'dearly beloved'.

Now at this point I can't help but remember those early versions of the *Sleeping Beauty* story with their necrophiliac 'heroes' (see p39) and wonder what this prince really intends to do with the coffin and the corpse. Also, it's important to point out that Snow White was only seven when the mirror announced that she had supplanted the queen in the beauty department. And, while an uncertain amount of time elapsed between that pronouncement and her death, it can't have been that long. So it's safe to assume that the beautiful corpse the prince wants to take possession of is that of a child between the ages of seven and eight.

Anyway, the dwarves agree to give him the coffin and he has his servants carry it away on their shoulders, but, as they stumble on some shrubs, the piece of poisoned apple so long stuck in Snow White's throat is dislodged and she comes alive again.

She's disorientated, as you'd imagine, but still says she'll go with the prince to his kingdom and be his wife.

The stepmother is invited to the wedding, though she doesn't know who the bride is until she consults her mirror.

Again, Snow White has cheated death, and now she's marrying a prince… the stepmother is beside herself. She decides she'll go along anyway – for she must identify the bride for herself.

At the wedding, the stepmother is punished for all she has done to Snow White by being made to wear red-hot iron shoes that have been heated over the fire. She 'dances' in these until she falls down dead.

CINDERELLA

Another victim of an ineffectual father's poor choice in a second wife is Cinderella. But her real problem is her new stepsisters. Her story was brought to a wide audience by Charles Perrault in 1697 – and this remains the foundation tale for subsequent tellings.

Here the father remarries a woman who is described as 'proud and haughty', who brings with her two (not three) daughters who are just like her. These sisters, Cinderella's primary taunters, are not described as ugly in appearance, only in behaviour to Cinderella, they are just not as virtuous and pretty as their new step-sibling. They nickname her Cinderbum or Cinderella because, under their mother's new regime, she is consigned to the kitchen as a domestic drudge where she must sit among the cinders of the fireplace when her work is done.

When it is announced that the prince is holding a ball, the two sisters are wildly excited and enlist Cinderella to help them with their dresses and hair – mocking her all the while.

When they've gone to the ball, Cinderella's godmother, a fairy, arrives to find her crying because she too wants to go to the ball. Her godmother not only sorts her out with a fabulous outfit but also transforms a pumpkin into a coach, six mice into horses, a rat into a driver and lizards into footmen – all with the proviso that she has to leave by midnight before her finery returns to rags.

At the ball she is the centre of attention, especially the prince's. She sits with her stepsisters, who do not recognise her, and exchanges pleasantries with them. She slips away at midnight and is back in her place in the kitchen when the two return, telling her all about the beautiful princess they met.

There is a ball the next night – and again she and the prince spend most of the evening together. She enjoys herself so much, in fact, that she forgets the rule about the midnight hour, and has to dash away in such haste that she loses a shoe, a glass slipper, in transit.

When the sisters return, Cinderella learns that the prince spent the rest of the ball moping and gazing at her shoe. They suggest that the prince must be in love with this mysterious princess.

And they are right, a few days later, it is announced that the prince will marry the girl the shoe fits. The slipper test is done properly – according to social rank. First princesses are tried, then duchesses, then all the other ladies of the court – but to no avail. When the sisters try the slipper and it doesn't fit, Cinderella pipes up and asks if she may have a turn. This causes her sisters great mirth but we're told that the gentleman tasked with the shoe-fitting exercise decides to let her try seeing as she's beautiful, despite her clothes and general presentation.

Of course the slipper fits perfectly, and she slips the second from her pocket and puts that on too. Her fairy godmother appears and with a tap of her wand transforms her rags into a splendid dress. Finally recognising her as the 'princess' from the ball, the two sisters prostrate themselves at her feet and beg forgiveness for their poor treatment of her. And virtuous Cinderella dispenses absolution. Not only that, but when she is married to the prince she arranges for these sisters to live at the palace, and even finds two lords for them to marry. Her father and stepmother are not mentioned again.

When things get ugly

Perrault's version is pretty gentle relative to both earlier and later tellings of the tale. In the Grimms' *Aschenputtel* from 1812, the heroine is blessed by her mother from her deathbed and so has God and her mother's spirit on her side for the trials ahead. And they are manifold.

The girl goes to her mother's grave every day and weeps, while her father recovers considerably faster and takes a new wife. One with two daughters, who are again 'beautiful and fair' but have 'wicked hearts'. They take away their new sister's nice clothes, give her an old smock and wooden shoes to wear and put her to work. They take great pleasure in relentlessly mocking her and set her tedious tasks such as picking peas and lentils out of the ashes of the fireplace, having poured them there for no other reason than to reinforce the drudgery of her new life. They take away her bed and make her sleep among the ashes of the hearth too – giving her the cruel moniker 'Aschenputtel' meaning 'Ashfool'.

One day, their father is going to a fair and asks his stepdaughters and daughter what gift they would like brought back to them. The stepdaughters request beautiful dresses, jewels and pearls. While the meek and mild Aschenputtel asks him, rather bizarrely, to break off the first twig that brushes off his hat on his way home and bring it to her. He goes off and duly gets the elaborate gifts for his stepdaughters and a hazel twig for Aschenputtel – which she duly plants on her mother's grave, watering it with her own tears. A tree grows and the girl continues to visit the grave/tree daily to weep and pray. But now the tree attracts a white bird – which grants her wishes.

When it is announced that the king of the land is holding a three-day festival for the specific purpose of finding a bride for his son, the prince, the sisters call on Aschenputtel to beautify them. She desperately wants to go too and asks her stepmother for permission. The cold-hearted woman initially says no, then sets a task for Aschenputtel – saying that she'll let her go to the festival if she completes it. She pours a bowl of lentils into the ashes by the fire and tells the girl that if she can take them all out in two hours she's free to attend.

Aschenputtel calls on her bird friends to assist – and duly two white pigeons, then two turtledoves, then many more birds fly in and set to work on the ashes. They complete the task in under an hour and so Aschenputtel goes to her stepmother to confirm her permission. But the stepmother has other ideas and sets her another task – this time it's two bowls-worth of lentils to be retrieved from the ashes in just one hour. Again the birds assist and complete the task, but again the stepmother reneges on her promise – this time for good.

The stepmother and stepsisters head off to the palace, leaving Aschenputtel to weep by her mother's graveside. She then makes a wish and her white bird friend throws her a fabulous dress of silver and gold, with shoes to match, from its perch on the magic hazel tree.

When she arrives at the ball, her stepfamily take her for some foreign princess from another land and watch as the prince dances with her all night. When it comes time to leave, the prince wants to escort her home, but instead Aschenputtel runs off. He follows her to see her disappear into her father's bird house. He approaches the father and the bird house is toppled only to find that nobody is in it. The father briefly suspects that the mystery woman could have been Aschenputtel, until he sees her in her usual place by the hearth.

The next day, Aschenputtel repeats her trick with the bird and the tree and is gifted with an even more elaborate dress. Again, the prince dances only with her, before she flees from him and disappears up a pear tree in her father's garden. Again, the father wonders if it could be his daughter and he topples this tree for the prince, but the maiden is nowhere to be found.

On the third day, the bird presents her with a magnificent dress and pure gold slippers. She dances all night with the prince but this time he has a plan to catch her if she runs off again and has coated the stairs of the palace to trap her – like a fly on fly-paper.

But all he gets is one of her gold shoes. Upon finding it, he declares he will marry the girl the shoe fits. News of this declaration spreads and, at their mother's behest, the stepsisters cup off a big toe and a heel, respectively, to try to squeeze their feet into the dainty slipper. But the large amount of blood in both instances gives the game away.

When the prince asks the father if he has any other daughters, he says no, only his dead wife's daughter who he says is 'deformed'. Nice guy.

The prince says he wants to see her despite the protestations of both father and stepmother.

She tries the shoe, which fits, and looking into her face the prince recognises his 'true bride'. The two ride off, much to the horror of her stepmother and stepsisters.

On the day of the wedding, the sisters come to try to curry favour with Aschenputtel – only to have their eyes pecked out by their stepsister's pigeon friends, and so, unlike Perrault's sisters, they are punished in rather horrific fashion for their malicious cruelty.

The Cat Cinderella and Rashin Coatie

In the pre-Perrault *La Gatta Cenerentola* (The Cat Cinderella) by Giambattista Basile from 1634, the story is similar in substance but also a lot darker. Indeed, in this telling, the heroine, known as Zezolla, is a killer.

When her widower father marries a 'wicked jade' who mistreats her terribly, Zezolla turns to her governess for advice. This lady prompts her to kill the stepmother by breaking her neck with the lid of a clothes chest. She is duly dispatched, but this does not end Zezolla's problems; instead, she is a pawn in the governess's own evil game. The governess manipulates Zezolla into getting her father to marry her – and then reveals she has not two, not three, but six previously undisclosed daughters.

The daughters move in and Zezolla is demoted to kitchen maid with her father's full complicity. He happily describes her as a 'graceless simpleton' to the king who seeks her out for the slipper-trial after the usual enchanted gowns and balls action.

The 'ugly sisters' motif is found in a Scottish version of the story, *Rashin Coatie*, recorded by Andrew Lang in 1878. And there are three of them. In this story, the heroine is made to wear a Rashin Coatie (coat of rushes) by her ugly stepsisters – and, rather than a ball, the girl makes her dramatic appearances to catch the prince's eye at church. Instead of a fairy godmother or a magic bird, she has a red calf gifted to her by her dear departed mother, who continues to help her even after her stepmother has it killed. Again, there's a shoe-fitting motif, and, as in the Grimms' version, the ugly sisters cut off bits of their feet in the hope of cramming their big trotters into the dainty slipper. When Rashin Coatie arrives on the scene looking glorious, the shoe literally jumps on to her foot.

Regaining her 'rightful' place

Despite the emphasis on Cinderella's selfless virtue and enchanting her 'prince charming' in the various tellings of this tale, the story is more about inheritance, displacement and social position than anything else. These are issues that would have been front of mind for the so-called *'précieuses'*, the French lady storytellers and writers who started the fairy-tale fashion in late seventeenth-century France and informed Perrault's work.

The story highlights how precarious the social position of a young woman, even from the upper classes, can be when a stepfamily moves in. Without legal or financial security, such a young woman has to be hugely resourceful or beautiful to regain her 'rightful' place in society. But in her behaviour she must be the very picture of humility, docility and grace.

Why does Cinderella so desperately want to go to a ball where prospective brides for a prince are effectively showcasing themselves? It's not simply because girls love dressing up. Given the oppressiveness of her home life, she takes a huge risk in attending, all the while racing against the midnight clock. This is a young woman on a mission, in defiance of her appalling stepfamily.

Reality bites

In contrast to *Cinderella*, *The Little Match Girl* by Hans Christian Andersen addresses the reality of impoverishment and class issues. In this 1845 tale, the tragic heroine is sent out on to the freezing streets on New Year's Eve night by her poverty-stricken parents to sell matches so that they might have a little money for food.

Exhausted and chilled to the bone, and not being able to sell a single match, she takes shelter in a nook between houses rather than return home empty-handed and face her father's blows. In her nook, she dreams of a better life – of a warm stove, then a beautiful Christmas tree and splendid holiday feast. She keeps striking matches to keep her visions alive a little longer and to get what little warmth she can from them.

She sees a shooting star and recalls how her grandmother, the only person who loved her, had once told her that a shooting star means that somebody has died. She then imagines her grandmother taking her by the arm and the two of them flying away from the cold, hunger and anxiety of life on earth. And with this last vision, she dies.

All the fantastical things this poor girl dreams of are just that – dreams. Whereas, in the world of *Cinderella*, they become reality for the poor little rich girl, deposed from her rightful place.

HANSEL AND GRETEL

> 'Hansel and Gretel is really scary.'
> – Kate Power, aged 7

Earlier, we met the diminutive Hop o' My Thumb (p167) from Charles Perrault's 1697 tale whose parents abandoned him and his brothers in the darkest depths of the woods when the going got tough, and welcomed them back when they returned with riches. While the blood-thirsty ogre in that story was pretty daunting, he is left in the shade by the truly sinister, cannibalistic witch in her gingerbread house in this later Grimm Brothers tale from 1812.

While it is the husband who suggests ditching the kids to a disgusted wife in *Hop o' My Thumb*, it is Hansel and Gretel's mother who proposes abandoning their two when hunger strikes and famine devastates the land. She's really very keen on the idea, chastising her husband as a 'fool' for not initially agreeing with her plan. As mentioned earlier, the Grimms changed their later version of this tale so that this woman was not their mother, but their stepmother – once again reinforcing that stereotype.

The children overhear this plotting and can't sleep for fear of what's ahead. But the more pragmatic of the two, Hansel, comforts his sister, saying he'll find a way out of it. Just like Hop before him, Hansel creeps out of the house and gathers white pebbles to use for a trail home.

The two are brought into the wood and told to stay put by a fire while their parents gather wood. After a long time alone, they fall asleep and awake utterly alone in the darkness. It is then that Hansel reveals his pebble scheme. They make their way home, arriving in the early morning only to be greeted by their stepmother chastising them for sleeping so long in the woods and failing to return home. A flimsy lie if ever there was one.

Undeterred, when hard times hit with renewed force a short while after, the stepmother again suggests that they abandon the children in the woods, but this time taking them to a deeper part so they cannot find their way out again. And the father again protests feebly before capitulating.

Again, the children hear the plotting and Hansel heads out to gather his guiding pebbles, but like his predecessor Hop finds that this time the door has been locked. On their journey into the woods the next day, Hansel attempts to lay a trail of breadcrumbs. When they awake as before alone in the dark woods, Hansel finds the trail has been eaten up by birds. And so the two are truly lost. For three days, they wander, eating berries they pick, with little sleep and cannot find a way out of the woods. On the third day, they see a lovely white bird who guides them to a house made of bread, with cake for a roof and sugar for windows.

The two immediately start tucking into the house, and do not stop even when a chastising voice comes from within, saying:

> 'Nibble, nibble, I hear a mouse.
> Who's that nibbling at my house?'

They answer:

> 'The wind, the wind, it's very mild,
> Blowing like the Heavenly Child.'

When a very old woman appears, they are frightened, but her kind words soothe them and they follow her into the house where she feeds them milk, pancakes, apples and nuts. She then makes them up two nice clean beds to sleep in and we're told 'they thought they were in heaven'.

But anyone who knows the story knows that, in fact, they've crossed the threshold into that other place... hell.

The reader is told that the kindly old woman is a wicked witch who is intent on killing, cooking and eating these abandoned siblings. When she looks in on them sleeping, she remarks to herself what a tasty meal they'll make.

She grabs Hansel and locks him up, screaming, behind

a grilled door. Then she turns to Gretel – telling her that she's to help fatten up her brother so she can eat him.

Now witches have red eyes and poor eyesight and the resourceful Hansel takes full advantage of this. When she asks him to stick his finger out of this cage to let her see if he's fattening, he sticks out a bone instead. He continues this trick for a month, until eventually the witch, frustrated at how skinny he is, decides she's going to 'slaughter' and eat him the following day regardless.

The witch sets about making her preparations and gets the oven going. She asks Gretel to crawl into it to check if it's hot enough with the intention of closing the door and roasting her up to be eaten too. But Gretel senses that something is amiss and so pretends to not understand the witch's command forcing the old woman to demonstrate. Seizing her opportunity, Gretel pushes the witch into the oven and shuts the door upon her. 'The witch began to howl dreadfully, but Gretel ran away, and the godless witch burned to death.'

She then releases Hansel and the two celebrate their freedom before helping themselves to the witch's treasures. They take as many pearls and jewels as they can carry and head off. They walk for hours until they come to a river with no crossing – and there they ask a white duck for assistance. The duck obliges and the two mount its back and it takes them across. Finally, they hit familiar territory and are soon on home ground.

Their father is overjoyed to see them, and luckily for them his wife has died in the meantime – but even if she hadn't one would imagine she'd be happy enough to see them too and their pockets' full of witch's booty.

Grisly origins for a grisly tale
In the early fourteenth century (between 1315 and 1322), Europe was struck by a famine that swept across the land from Russia in the east to Italy in the southwest, and across the sea to Britain. Millions starved to death when crops failed for two years running. In addition to mass death, there was a rise in violent crime, and cannibalism, child abandonment and infanticide are thought to have occurred on an unprecedented scale.

It is surmised that this folk memory might have informed the *Hansel and Gretel* tale, where famine is openly referred to from the outset.

The tale is identical in parts to the *Hop o My Thumb* story, and it also shares many similarities with *Finette Cendron* or *Clever Cinders* (1721) by Madame d'Aulnoy. In this tale, the heroine manages to shove an ogre into an oven in much the same way that Gretel does the witch.

Some have interpreted the fact that the mother/step-mother dies before the children return home hints at the fact that she may either literally or metaphorically have been the same person as the witch.

(Too much) Makin' Whuppie

An interesting hybrid of the tale recorded by Joseph Jacobs for his 1890 publication *English Fairy Tales* is the tale *Molly Whuppie*. This story, which has Scottish, English and Irish roots, combines elements of *Hop o' My Thumb*, *Hansel and Gretel* and *Jack and the Beanstalk*.

In this story, a man and his wife have too many children and can't provide food for them all, so they decide to take the three youngest (all girls) off into the woods to abandon them there. Thoroughly lost, the three wander for hours until they see the light of a house.

The woman of the house greets them gruffly and says she can't help them as her husband is a giant and will kill them. But they beg to come in just for a little while and promise to leave before the giant returns. So she takes them in and gives them bread and milk. But then comes a great knock on the door and the familiar announcement:

> Fee, fie, fo, fum,
> I smell the blood of some earthly one.

The wife manages to protect the 'three poor lassies' – the canniest of whom is Molly Whuppie, the youngest – from her husband, who says they can stay the night. The three girls are put into the same bed as the giant's three daughters – you see where this is going…

Molly swaps the straw ropes she and her sisters have around their necks for the gold chains around the giant's daughters, and, when their father comes in the night with his club to do bloody murder unto them, he feels in the dark and so bludgeons the three girls with straw necklaces, i.e. his own children.

Molly and her sisters hightail it out of there and next find themselves at the grand house of a king. Molly relates their tale and the king tells her that, if she can steal the giant's sword, he will have his eldest son, a prince, marry her eldest sister.

A little like Jack of *Jack and the Beanstalk* fame, Molly slinks back into the giant's house and gets the sword while the giant is asleep and snoring. He awakes and gives chase but the girl gets away and returns to the king with her spoils.

Impressed, the king then says that, if she successfully steals the giant's ring, he'll give her his youngest son as a husband for herself.

And so the girl returns and waits until the giant is asleep, but, just as she's trying to slip the ring from his finger, he grabs hold of her. He asks her what she'd do to him if she was in his position. At which point she says, 'I would put you into a sack, and I'd put the cat inside wi' you, and the dog aside you, and a needle and thread and shears, and I'd hang you up upon the wall, and I'd go to the wood, and choose the thickest stick I could get, and I would come home, and take you down, and bang you till you were dead.'

'Well, Molly,' says the giant, 'I'll just do that to you.'

And so the giant puts Molly in the sack with these various accoutrements and heads off to get the stick to beat her to death with.

Molly then tricks the giant's wife into taking her place in the sack (remember that this woman had previously been kind to her) – when the giant returns he duly starts to beat the sack and cannot hear his wife's protestations over the howls of the dog and shrieks of the cat.

The giant then spies Molly by the back door and curses her. She runs off, marries the prince and never sees the giant again.

Whether the wife survived the beating in the bag, we're not told.

BLUEBEARD

I never read this tale as a child, but a few friends referred me to it as the one that scared the bejesus out of them in their formative years. And on reading it for the first time as an adult it's easy to see why.

Though it was included in Charles Perrault's collection of fairy tales in 1697 alongside *Cinderella, Rapunzel, Sleeping Beauty* et al, it remains on the peripheries of the canon shared with modern-day children.

Jack Zipes sees the *Bluebeard* story as the most influential story about a serial killer, referring to it as a 'master narrative' of that genre. It also draws on some of the oldest and best-known biblical stories – that of Adam and Eve and how a woman's curiosity leads to her downfall. Ditto Pandora's Box. In terms of what it tells young readers about marriage – well, it certainly advises extreme caution in choosing a prospective mate.

Perrault's story starts conventionally enough. We are introduced to a rich man with many houses and treasures but who is blighted by a physical issue that renders him unattractive to the majority – his inexplicable blue beard. We then learn that he has been married many times, but that nobody knows what became of his wives. When he feels it's time to marry again, he earmarks two sisters to woo and invites them to one of his grand country houses.

There they are entertained in fine style – wined, dined and entertained – until the younger of the two sisters softens and decides that marriage to this man may not be all bad.

So they marry, and after a month Bluebeard tells his young bride he must go away on business. He entrusts her with a huge set of keys to all the various rooms of his vast home. But he warns her that there is one room that she must not enter – this is his private room and is tucked away in the bowels of the house.

Of course, no sooner has he departed than her curiosity

to see inside this room starts to gnaw at her. She makes her way to the forbidden chamber in such a hurry that she nearly falls and breaks her neck. Upon unlocking the door, she sees a sight of unimaginable horror – all of Bluebeard's former wives are here, dead and tied up along the walls, while the floor is awash with their blood. In fright, she drops the key on the bloody floor.

When her husband returns early and asks for his keys back, he sees the blood on the key to the forbidden room, which his wife was unable to remove, though she scrubbed and scrubbed. The secret is out and he condemns her to death.

She manages to beg ten minutes from him to say some final prayers – and uses this to signal to the outside world from a high tower. It just so happens that her brothers are en route and she just needs a little longer to allow them to get there in time to save her. So she stalls and stalls again.

They arrive in the nick of time, just as Bluebeard is about to chop his wife's head off. They dispatch the villain immediately.

As Bluebeard had no heirs, this latest wife inherits all his vast wealth. She marries a much nicer man and manages to forget all about the 'bad time' she had with her murderous first husband.

Perrault assigns two morals to this tale. The first is a warning about curiosity. As in the Bible, it's ultimately the woman's fault for not obeying God/her husband.

His second one is a little more playful, showing that, while women should still ideally obey 'the master of the house', times are changing:

> People with sense who use their eyes,
> Study the world and know its ways,
> Will not take long to realise
> That this is a tale of bygone days,
> And what it tells is now untrue:
> Whether his beard is black or blue,
> The modern husband does not ask
> His wife to undertake a task
> Impossible for her to do,
> And even when dissatisfied,
> With her he's quiet as a mouse.
> It isn't easy to decide
> Which is the master in the house.

Where fact meets fiction

There are a few theories about the origin of the Bluebeard story – one associated with a real-life serial killer.

Gilles de Montmorency-Laval (also known as Gilles de Rais or Baron de Rais, 1404–40) was a Breton knight who fought alongside Joan of Arc. However, he is best known for his penchant for murdering children. Indeed, it is thought that his victims number anywhere between eighty and two hundred, between the ages of six and eighteen and of both genders. Certainly, the bodies of forty children were uncovered at one site at Machecoul near Nantes. He claimed to have burned a substantial number of other bodies and to have had assistance in procuring, killing and disposal. The details in his confession about rape, torture and dismembering of children are pretty difficult reading.

After a lengthy trial, he was hanged for his crimes at Nantes in October 1440.

Another Brittany connection is with the story of Conomor the Accursed (or Cursed) and his wife Tréphine. Conomor was a real-life Breton king in the early medieval period (mid-sixth century). Known for his great cruelty, the story goes that he murdered three of his wives when they became pregnant before marrying his fourth, Tréphine. She initially refused to marry him but finally assented when he threatened to invade her father's land. When Conomor was away, she visited a room containing relics and the belongings of his murdered wives. There, their ghosts appeared to Tréphine, warning her that her husband would kill her if she too became pregnant, because of his fear of a prophecy that he would be killed by his own son. Tréphine was indeed pregnant and so fled in fear when her husband returned and she gave birth in a forest. She managed to hide her infant son before her husband caught up with her and beheaded her. But, because of her pious ways, Saint Gildas is said to have found her and restored her to life.

Subsequently she lived together with her son, Trémeur, but upon her death Conomor once more appeared and killed his son.

The fierce Conomor is also thought to be the model for the mythological giant Cormoran from *Jack the Giant Killer* (p164).

CONCLUSION

'If you want your children to be intelligent, read
them fairy tales. If you want them to be more
intelligent, read them more fairy tales.'

– Albert Einstein

In the introduction, I mentioned recent surveys done in
the USA and the UK, which indicate that parents are
starting to turn away from traditional nursery rhymes and
fairy tales in favour of contemporary songs and stories.

But if fairy tales are in decline for today's children,
they're in the ascent for adults. The latter half of the
twentieth century saw writers like Margaret Atwood
(*Bluebeard's Egg*) and Angela Carter (*The Bloody Chamber*)
use or subvert the fairy-tale genre to explore sexuality,
especially female sexuality, in new ways. They turned

on its head the woman-as-passive-victim model found in many of the tales, compounded by the Disney-fication of fairy tales since *Snow White and the Seven Dwarves* hit the big screen in 1937. And there has been a steady stream of adult retellings ever since, including fantasy novels, erotic fiction and racy Manga comic versions.

The last few years have seen a slew of fairy tale and related fantasy stories for teenage and adult audiences on both big and small screens. Again, Angela Carter was a pioneer of the fairy tale reimagined for screen. In 1984, she worked with director Neil Jordan on *The Company of Wolves*, a 'gothic fantasy' film that brought together elements of her three *Little Red Riding Hood*-inspired short stories from her collection *The Bloody Chamber*.

Since then, the Little Red story has been innovatively reimagined from *Freeway* (1996) starring Reese Wither-spoon as Vanessa, a deprived teenager up against serial killer Bob Wolverton (Kiefer Sutherland), to *Red Riding Hood* (2011), which drops the 'Little' and sees Amanda Seyfried don the red cloak in a werewolf tale crammed with brooding hunks and leather doublets.

In 2012, Snow White got a makeover in *Snow White and the Huntsman*, becoming a Joan of Arc-type warrior maiden played by *Twilight* star Kristen Stewart, with Charlize Theron playing the evil queen, her arch nemesis. *Hansel & Gretel: Witch Hunters*, in 2013, had the once-abandoned brother and sister as a dynamic duo of crossbow-toting hired killers, travelling the land exterminating wicked witches. The list goes on…

As well as the detective series *Grimm* mentioned earlier, TV has recently given us *Beauty and the Beast*, an updated version of another series from 1987, in which a detective, Catherine Chandler, witnesses her mother's murder and is saved from death herself by a 'beast' called Vincent, an ex-army man who has an Incredible Hulk-like problem of transforming into a beastly creature under duress because of a mutation in his DNA caused by an experiment. Obviously, they fall in love despite this.

Then there's *Once Upon a Time*, a series set in the town of Storybrooke, Maine, whose residents are characters from various fairy tales who have been transported to the 'real world' town, unaware of their true identities. Here we find Snow White rubbing shoulders with the Evil Queen, Prince Charming and the Huntsman, as well as Rumpelstiltskin, Pinocchio, Red Riding Hood, Aurora (*Sleeping Beauty*), Ariel (*The Little Mermaid*), Belle (Beauty from *Beauty and the Beast*), the warrior maiden Mulan (originally in a sixth-century Chinese ballad more recently made famous by Disney), Robin Hood and Captain Hook from *Peter Pan*. There's plenty of inter-story romance and, in a thoroughly modern twist, Mulan is gay and in love with Princess Aurora.

Having every conceivable mythological character and/or creature in a series has been an approach in US

TV since *Buffy the Vampire Slayer* burst on to screens in 1997, followed shortly thereafter by the 'wiccan' sisters in *Charmed* (1998). More recently, there's been *Lost Girl*, an ongoing Canadian series about the race of 'Fae' (as in Faeries) who live alongside us oblivious humans. The show is populated with creatures taken from folklores across the world, fairy tales, religion and mythology. The main character is a Succubus (female demon from medieval lore) called Bo, who likes to have sex, a lot, with both men and women.

It remains to be seen whether fairy tales and nursery rhymes in their traditional form will be seen as relevant or suitable for children in the future. Whatever we think about them and their strange messages – they represent thousands of years of human storytelling and are one of the few tangible legacies we have from our remote ancestors.

So many have already become artefacts and curiosities, kept alive only in scholarly books and articles. The future of the 'canon' tales rests with individual parents, in individual households – a long way from their communal, oral origins.

Whether these archetypal stories continue to be passed to future generations is up to us…

INDEX OF RHYMES AND TALES

INDEX OF RHYMES AND TALES

INDEX OF RHYMES AND TALES

BIBLIOGRAPHY

Alchin, Linda *The Secret History of Nursery Rhymes* (Nielson, 2013)

Andersen, Hans Christian *Hans Christian Andersen's Fairy Tales* (Acheron Press, 2012. Kindle Edition)

Anonymous reporter 'Fairytales too scary for modern children, say parents' (*Daily Telegraph*, 12 Feb 2012)

Anonymous reporter 'Pop songs at bedtime push out lullabies: Parents opt for lyrics from Adele and Rihanna to send babies off to sleep' (*Daily Mail*, 11 November 2013)

Bettelheim, Bruno *The Uses of Enchantment: The Meaning and Importance of Fairy Tales* (Vintage Books, 1976)

Berdichevsky, Norman *Hans Christian Andersen's 'Fairy Tales' for Adults* (New English Review, September 2007)

Brothers Grimm *The Complete Fairy Tales* (Vintage, 2007)

Bunce, John Thackray *Fairy Tales, Their Origin and Meaning, 1878* (Amazon, 2013)

Carter, Angela *The Bloody Chamber and Other Stories* (Vintage Digital; New Ed edition, 2012. Kindle Edition)

Evans, Stephen *Are Grimms' Fairy Tales too twisted for children?* (BBC Culture, 1 August 2013)

Jack, Albert *Pop Goes the Weasel: The Secret Meanings of Nursery Rhymes* (Penguin, 2008. Kindle Edition)

Lawson, Mark 'Cape fear' (*The Guardian*, 27 September 2006)

McMillan, Graeme 'Another bite of the poisoned apple: Why does pop culture love fairy tales again?' (*Time*, 30 May 2012)

Opie, Iona and Peter *The Classic Fairy Tales* (Oxford University Press, 1974)

Opie, Iona and Peter (eds) *The Oxford Dictionary of Nursery Rhymes* (Oxford University Press, 1997)

Orenstein, Catherine *Little Red Riding Hood Uncloaked: Sex, Morality, and the Evolution of a Fairy Tale* (Basic Books, 2003)

Perrault, Charles *The Complete Fairy Tales* (Oxford University Press, 2009. Kindle Edition)

Pullman, Philip *Grimm Tales: For Young and Old* (Penguin, 2012)

Warner, Marina *From the Beast to the Blonde: On Fairy Tales and Their Tellers* (Vintage, 1995)

Zipes, Jack *The Enchanted Screen: The Unknown History of Fairy-Tale Films* (Routledge, 2011. Kindle Edition)

BIBLIOGRAPHY

Zipes, Jack *The Irresistible Fairy Tale: The Cultural and Social History of a Genre* (Princeton University Press, 2012. Kindle Edition)

CONTENTS

s in 2019
olishing Group

Carlton Books Limited 2019

this publication my be
val system, or transmitted,
without the prior written
or otherwise circulated in
other than that in which it is
ar condition being imposed on

s book is available from the

First

An i

20 M

Lonc

Text

All ri

repro

in any

permi

any fo

publis

the su

A CIP

British

ISBN 9

Printed

INTRODUCTION

Rugby is a sport whose defining characteristics include raw passion, brutal honesty and comradeship, all of which are underpinned by an often savage wit. It's a combination which has produced some of the best bon-mots in the sporting world, and none more so than when it comes to the cradle of the game: England.

Whether it comes from the fans, referees, coaches or players, rugby humour is often as high-octane and hard-hitting as the biggest tackle in the heat of a Twickenham international. Whether it's an entertaining case of foot in mouth disease or a withering put-down of a teammate or opponent, there is something for everyone in these pages.

One of my favourites in *The Pocket Book of England Rugby* was Damian Hopley's immortal quip after he heard he was being touted as England's answer to Jonah Lomu ("Me? As England's answer to Jonah Lomu? Joanna Lumley, more likely.") but there are quotes which changed the game too.

When Will Carling talked about the RFU's "57 old farts", for instance, it was an off-camera aside but it came to symbolize much that was wrong with the game and was a catalyst for profound change in the way the game is run.

For those who love Rugby Union, *The Pocket Book of England Rugby*'s verbal treasures will transport you straight back to the games and controversies of the past in a way that no dry history of the game is able to do.

So we hope that you enjoy reading the wit and occasional shards of wisdom in the following pages as much as I enjoyed putting it together.

CHAPTER 1

SWING LOW, SWEET CHARIOT

"I do hope not."

Captain **CARL AARVOLD**, replies to a fan who said, "may the better team win", before England met South Africa in 1932